ENDORSEMENTS

Today's postmodern culture demands we present Christ in a way people can identify with and understand. *Soulmate* is that kind of read! This edgy, direct, relevant, but clear story will produce positive eternal outcomes.

—Dr. George Cope
Pastoral Director, Vision Orlando

So many people settle for an average, humdrum relationship with God. In *Soulmate*, Dexter Sanders calls us into the deep—to follow the longings of our heart, to get in touch with how badly we want intimacy, and to challenge the status quo. He encourages us to say, "I'm all in; I want all that God has for me!"

—Bob Lenz
President, Life Promotions
Appleton, Wisconsin

A peek inside these pages will quickly provide a clear path to obtaining a closer relationship with God. Using his pen as a sword where others would shy away, Dexter boldly employs a practical, familiar subject to catapult cutting-edge revelation essential to spiritual maturity. Prepare to be blessed!

—Bishop Allen T.D. Wiggins
Senior Pastor, The Hope Church
Orlando, Florida

T0099655

Soulmate

Soulmate

Your Ultimate Relationship Awaits

Dexter Sanders

HIGHERLIFE
PUBLISHING & MARKETING, INC.

Oviedo, Florida

Dedication

This book is dedicated to my parents, Warner Lee and the late Flossie Mae Sanders. God has blessed me to share the life-changing gospel of Jesus Christ all over this country and abroad. None of this would have been possible without the love, care and support you gave to Adan, Alisa, Diane, Susie and me.

During the lowest moments in my life, without the things the two of you instilled, I could have never survived.

Dad, you taught me about the importance of having Jesus Christ in my life, as well as the notion that success is only achieved through hard work. Just know that your work in me has not been in vain.

Mom, you made me understand that I could achieve anything; you believed in me. I just wish you were here to see this day.

Thank you for making me go to church every Sunday. Thank you for insisting I go to college. Thank you for working me so hard and making me understand that I could be better and do more. Thank you for providing the greatest introduction in the world, to my Lord and Savior Jesus Christ.

Without the two of you, this book would never touch the world, but because it will, many lives will be changed and many souls saved, all because of you.

Thanks Mom and Dad!!!!

WARNING

The contents of this book may rock your preconceived ideas about God and your religious tradition. Read at your own risk.

The thoughts and ideas presented in this book may be hazardous to your beliefs, resulting in more fulfillment and joy than you dreamed possible. Any reference to an intimate physical relationship is offered in order to help you embrace a deeper spiritual truth.

A Personal Note
From the Author

I am passionate about wanting you to embrace a more vibrant and intimate relationship with God. This is why I wrote this book. I realize that people in the church often talk about God in ways that seem mystical, foreign, and just not very relatable to the average person.

This book uses the illustration of a human relationship to help you consider and understand what might actually be possible for you in knowing and enjoying God more fully. But I'll warn you, in the last couple chapters I get pretty real in talking about the more intimate ways God wants to interact with us. It freaks out a lot of church people.

Frankly, even my publisher is concerned. But my hope is that you hang in there with me, and trust that I'm not trying to teach you something weird. I'm not trying to bring the glory of a spiritual relationship down to just a fleshly or human level but rather use what we experience on a human level to believe what is possible on a spiritual level. Hopefully reading this book will be for you the beginning of an incredible journey with God.

Table of Contents

Foreword

God came to Earth to invite us, personally, into a relationship. And while Christians at times downplay relationships, Evangelist Dexter Sanders is completely sold on the idea.

In *Soulmate* he asks, Have you ever experienced an empty feeling inside of you? It can be so strong, kind of like an itch that you can't scratch. No matter how hard you try to get at it, you can't.

Dexter has experienced such a feeling. However, he says that emptiness inside gave God the room to speak to him concerning the things that he needed in his life. To his dismay, God explained to him that the empty feeling he was experiencing was actually his soul crying out for God.

Dexter gives Moses and David as biblical examples of those who have experienced this empty feeling in times past and filled it through developing a relationship with God. The current generation is driven by a God-given desire to know others and to be known by others. In seeking to connect in meaningful ways, most of them have found a place of belonging that is outside the organized church. Why not bring the two together?

Those who are sold out to relationships can teach Christians how to be better friends to people who need God. It's time for relationship to be restored to the heart of the gospel. And when that happens, can revival be far behind?

Dexter invites us to see "relationship" not as something "out there," but as something within. The key, needless to say, lies in pulling the right lesson from each bad relationship. And he is superb at it.

Dr. Henry Vernon

Senior Servant

New Ebenezer Christian Church

Kissimmee, Florida

Acknowledgments

First and foremost, I want to acknowledge Yahweh, the God of Abraham, Isaac, and Jacob, the God of our Lord and Savior, Yeshua the Christ. Thank you for loving me.

To my wife Camille, thank you for the love and support you've given me and for being a loving mother.

To my four sons: Corey, Terrell, Justin, and Blake. You guys are my inspiration.

To my brother and sisters: Adan, Alisa, Diane, and Susie. I love you!

To "my girls," the office staff: Natalia (Ne Ne), Belinda (Bebe), and Liana (Lele). You girls make it happen.

To my *Soulmate* funding team: Art and Bonnie Ally, Jack and Charo Berry, Dean and Jane Blakenship, Scott and Joanie Cahill, Michael and Kitty O'Grody, and Rock Orlando Center of Transformation. This could not have happened without you.

To Mother Barbara Bey. Thanks for your editing skills, but more importantly for your love and prayers.

To Dr. Henry Vernon. Thanks for always being there for me.

To Scott Cahill. Thank you for being my friend.

To the preordained people whose lives will be changed as a result of reading *Soulmate*. God loves you!

Introduction

For centuries, humans have looked upon God as a mystical, even illusional, being that is all so removed from our everyday existence. Even if we accept that He really exists, we don't think of God as our Father but instead a being so big, so powerful that there's no way He could be a very personal God. We don't think we can talk to Him. We don't believe that He's the kind of God that would respond if we called out to Him.

Many have concluded that God is simply out of reach and out of touch. If they were really honest with themselves, most Christians would say that they don't have a close relationship with God. We toss the concept around in our religious circles, but if we were pushed to tell the truth we'd likely have to admit that a personal relationship with God is something we can't really grasp. Yet the entire Christian faith hinges on the belief that God is so personal that He came down from glory to be in relationship with us in a very personal way.

One of the reasons God came to earth in the form of a man named Jesus was so that we could know that we can have a personal relationship with Him, in the same manner we have relationships with other humans, so that we can approach Him like we approach any other man, even though He is God Almighty. If this is true, we don't need to change the way we talk to communicate with God. We don't need to change the way we dress to get God's attention, and we don't have to talk in riddles or rhymes for God to notice us. We can talk to God the same way we talk to a loved one but at the same time being careful to speak with reverence, respect, and humility.

There are those who have come up through a church tradition that suggests they must alter the pronunciation of words, and amplify or quiet, augment or diminish their voice when communicating with God.

However, the Bible says that we can simply talk to God the way we would our earthly father or a friend.

Exodus 33:11 reads: *"So the Lord spoke to Moses face to face, as a man speaks to his friend. And he would return to the camp, but his servant Joshua the son of Nun, a young man, did not depart from the tabernacle."*

This example of Moses and his communication with God is given to us so that we can understand that we, too, can be in relationship with God in a very personal way.

Have you ever experienced an empty feeling inside of you? It can be so strong, kind of like an itch that you can't scratch. No matter how hard you try to get at it, you can't. I have experienced such a feeling. However, that emptiness that was inside me gave God room to speak to me concerning the things that I needed in my life. To my dismay, God explained to me that the empty feeling I was experiencing was actually my soul crying out for Him.

Introduction

It's the same thing that happens when you are a baby. You can't talk; the only way you know to communicate is to cry out. No one taught you how to cry, it was just something that you came into this world doing. So whenever you were in need, you cried out. When you did, you didn't just cry out for anybody. You cried out for your mother. Even fresh from the womb, you cried out for your mother because you knew she was the one who carried you. It was Mother who fed you. It was Mother who loved you even while you were yet in her womb. As you began to grow, whenever you were hungry you continued to call out for Mother. When you were wet or soiled, you cried out for your mother.

Your spirit is the same way. Even while you were still in your mother's womb, your spirit was crying out for the Father. Whenever your spirit is not getting what it needs, it cries out. Just as you cried out to your mother when you were a baby in need, when your spirit is in need it cries out to the Father. It wants to be close to the Father.

In Psalm 42:1–3 we read:

> *"As the deer pants for the water brooks, so pants my soul for You, O God. My soul thirsts for God, for the living God. When shall I come and appear before God? My tears have been my food day and night, while they continually say to me, 'Where is your God?'"*

Here King David cries out that his soul "thirsts for God." Most of us have never really known what it is to physically thirst for water. Unless you have been stranded in the desert or some other situation where it was not available, chances are you don't know what it is to thirst for it. To thirst means to desire, to long for, or to have a craving or hunger. In this Psalm, water is used as the object of desire, which suggests that there is a need because of dehydration or dryness in the body of the believer.

Putting those two meanings together, we come to understand that David was in need of hydration because he was dry. His dryness was not physical, however, but spiritual. His dryness caused a longing and hunger for the very thing that could satisfy his thirst. According to the scripture, the only thing that could take away the dryness and hydrate David's life was "the living God." David was clear to explain that it was his very soul that longed for God.

God created us to be in a fruitful, loving relationship with Him.

Many of us have experienced or are experiencing the same thing as David. There is this longing in our souls. There is a thirst way deep down inside that just won't go away. We try filling it with other things. We try filling it with other people. No matter what we try, though, we always come up dry. Sadly enough, many who come to this crossroad in life conclude that there is nothing better, so they resign themselves to an empty existence. This is not what God had in mind when He created us.

God created us to be in a fruitful, loving relationship with Him. He created us to love Him and to love one another the way He loves us. God desires to provide physical and spiritual water when

Introduction

we're thirsty and food when we're hungry. God wants to meet our every desire, which is the sole reason He has brought you to this book. Together we will explore the love of our God and His desire to be connected to us in the most intimate ways.

Yes, God wants to be in relationship with you. However, this examination will go a step further, to suggest that God wants to have a love affair with you! Having a love affair with God is no different than having one with any human, in some ways. The things it takes to start and maintain a relationship with a potential girlfriend or boyfriend, husband or wife are the same ones it takes to establish and maintain an affair with God.

There are steps that one must take when establishing a love relationship. When a man wants a woman, or a woman wants a man, social norms suggest the steps they must follow. It's very important to go through them in a particular order. Putting one step before another could trigger a negative domino effect, ending the relationship abruptly before it ever really gets started. The same is true when seeking a love affair with God. He is a God of order. He created the steps, so it's very important to adhere to them.

Before we get started, it's important to discuss the usage of the term "affair." Your immediate thought may generate negative emotions. A husband cheating on his wife is said to have had an affair. Two unmarried people engaging in sexual activity are said to be having an affair.

But to experience the spiritual blessings I believe God has prepared for you in the pages that follow, it is necessary to abandon every negative association society has given to this term and to begin to see it in a different light. The term "affair" will be used to express a loving, committed, intimate, and personal relationship between God and man.

Now let's journey and explore how you can have a love affair with God.

Step One:
The Rendezvous

If you are serious about having a love affair with God, you must first come into contact with Him. If you want a relationship with another person, it will never happen while you sit at home alone watching television. You have to position yourself to come into proximity of the other person.

What exactly does that mean? If you want to be in a relationship with someone who is an expert in law, you might want to hang around lawyers. If you want to come into a relationship with a person that plays basketball, you might want to go to a few basketball games. If you want a relationship with a Christian, you might want to take yourself to church. That being said, if you want a relationship with God, you might want to hang out where He is.

One of the truly great things about being in relationship with God is He makes it so easy, because God is everywhere.

Psalm 139:7–8 declares: *"Where can I go from Your Spirit? Or where can I flee from Your presence? If I ascend into heaven, You are there; if I make my bed in hell, behold, You are there."*

God is everywhere. God's presence is everywhere. So you may be thinking, "If God is everywhere, I'm already in His presence." This is true, you are always in God's physical presence, but His spiritual presence is a whole different ball game. Coming into the presence of God is a spiritual experience.

In Matthew 6:6, Jesus tells His disciples: *"But you, when you pray, go into your room, and when you have shut your door, pray to your Father who is in the secret place; and your Father who sees in secret will reward you openly."*

According to this passage, you can't go out to the club to find a love affair with God. According to scripture it is to be found in a secret place. That means it is a quiet place where God will meet you. All you have to do is make yourself available to meet Him. God will meet you in a secret place that He has reserved just for you. It's a spiritual place where your spirit will come into the presence of God's Spirit. When this happens you'll know because your life will never be the same. Anyone who meets God and dwells in the secret place of the Almighty can never be the same.

God would rather we not suffer in order to finally hear Him speak.

Psalm 91:1 says: *"He who dwells in the secret place of the Most High shall abide under the shadow of the Almighty."*

To be in God's presence requires our hearts to be open to hear Him. He's there all the time—we're just too busy to notice. Most times we are brought to the point where we can hear God through our struggles and problems. This is unfortunate because God would rather we not suffer in order to finally hear Him speak.

I grew up in a Baptist church and, as far as I understood, I was a Christian. My parents took me to church every Sunday. I sang in the choir. I was on the usher board. My father was a deacon, and my mother was on the mother board, in addition to being the choir director. I thought I knew God and God knew me. I believed I had a good understanding of who Jesus was and the role He played in my life.

As an adult I wandered off into the world, experimenting with every type of woman, drug, and drink I could find. After years of drugging and drinking, I found myself out of control. Things got so bad that suicide became a serious consideration. Then I remembered what my father would say to me as a child. I couldn't recall the exact words, but it was centered around the notion that a life without Jesus is really not a life at all.

I began to call out to God in a way that I never had before. I knew I was destined to die a crackhead and an alcoholic. I knew God was my only hope. So I cried out with all I had. It didn't happen right away, but it did happen: God showed up in a mighty way and turned my life around. He also brought to my remembrance the many times He attempted to get my attention.

He showed me how time and time again He had tried to communicate with me, including the many times He tried to warn me, but I didn't listen. But because God desired to have a love affair with me, He allowed me to experience some things that would bring me to His feet, on my knees, begging for love. I found that secret place that God prepared for me in the midst of my drug addiction.

Some might wonder, how can a drug addict come into the presence of God? It's a question that seems appropriate in the light of Psalm 140:13: *"Surely the righteous shall give thanks to Your name; the upright shall dwell in Your presence."*

You would probably agree that a drug addict or alcoholic does not exactly meet the criteria of the "upright." So it was a good thing for me that God was not measuring whether I was upright based on my behavior. The fact of the matter is, God was not looking at my inability to stay sober. He was not looking at my lying, cheating, or stealing. God was not concerned about how I looked or how horrible I smelled. I was able to come into the presence of God by what was in my heart. He used pain and suffering as a way to bring me into His presence.

Exodus 2:23 says: *"Now it happened in the process of time that the king of Egypt died. Then the children of Israel groaned because of the bondage, and they cried out; and their cry came up to God because of the bondage."*

This account recalls a time of suffering for God's chosen people, the Israelites. They had been enslaved by the Egyptians for many years. After much pain and suffering, they groaned and cried out. I certainly can relate to that: it must have been much like the way I desperately groaned and cried out to God to save me from the bondage of crack cocaine.

Step One: The Rendezvous

The Israelites cried out to God. But look at what happened next. The Bible says "their cry came up to God." Their cry came into the presence of God. Reading to the end of verse 23, we find out why: "because of the bondage." What we can take away from this is the fact that, indeed, God hears us through our bondage.

Perhaps you are thinking, "I've never been a slave to anyone. I've never been in bondage." I would say to you that you may never have been enslaved like the Israelites, but if you are a human being then you have definitely been a slave to something. Bondage comes in many forms. For me it was drugs, alcohol, and sex. Some find themselves in bondage to other people, jobs, hobbies, and especially the love of money. But the good news is that no matter how much you may suffer at the hands of your bondage, God can hear you through it, as He did the Israelites.

Look at Exodus 2:24: *"So God heard their groaning, and God remembered His covenant with Abraham, with Isaac, and with Jacob."*

From the previous verse we learned that the cry of the Israelites came up to God. Now we see that their cry not only came into the presence of God, but that He also heard it. This tells us that your cry alone can move you into the presence of God, but God hearing your cry is another story. It's no different with us: many things come to our attention, but that does not mean we will, in turn, give our attention to all of them. In this case, God heard the Israelites' cry, and as a result of Him hearing it, He was moved to action. The last part of verse 24 tells that "God remembered His covenant with Abraham, with Isaac, and with Jacob."

If you are familiar with the story of Abraham, Isaac, and Jacob, you will know that God promised Abraham that He would be God to him and all his descendants.

In Genesis 17:7 God said: *"And I will establish My covenant between Me and you and your descendants after you in their generations, for an everlasting covenant, to be God to you and your descendants after you."*

For many of us, it will be through our suffering, through our problems, through our pain that the cries from our heart will enter into the presence of God. He will hear us and remember that we are His children and He is our God.

Though pain and struggles are necessary for most of us to enter into the presence of God, it's not true for everyone. There is one sure way that we can enter into God's presence on a more positive note. Psalm 100:1–5 declares:

> *Make a joyful shout to the Lord, all you lands! Serve the Lord with gladness; come before His presence with singing. Know that the Lord, He is God; it is He who has made us, and not we ourselves; we are His people and the sheep of His pasture. Enter into His gates with thanksgiving, and into His courts with praise. Be thankful to Him, and bless His name. For the Lord is good; His mercy is everlasting, and His truth endures to all generations.*

This describes one sure way we can come into the presence of God—through our praise and worship. The psalmist reminds us to come into His presence with singing, to enter His gates with thanksgiving. When we think about coming into a relationship with God, many of us are focused on what else God can do for us, thinking very little about what He has already done. This is probably because most of us can't recognize how God continued to bless and keep us even during the season when we had no desire at all to be in relationship with Him.

We don't stop to thank Him for having protected us while we were busy out in the world. When we finally hear God's call we show up expecting Him to do more. To come into the presence of God, we first need to recognize, appreciate, and praise Him for what He has already done in our lives. You have to acknowledge and understand that if it were not for the mercy and love of God, you would not even be in the position to experience Him more. It was His grace and mercy that afforded you the opportunity.

So it is in that quiet place where you will both hear from God and meet God. It's in that quiet place that God will begin to reveal to you His perfect plan for your life. There's nothing left to do but get in there and meet God.

He's waiting for you. It's the most amazing catch of all. It's like the most handsome man or the prettiest woman in the world waiting for you. It does not matter where you are in your life; whether you're on the brink of destruction or things are going rather well, if you're reading this book right now it's because God wants to connect with you. God is waiting to rendezvous with you.

What are you waiting for?

Step Two:

Recognize: "He's So Fine"

You have probably heard this sentiment expressed before. When a woman sees an attractive man she may say, "Oh, he's so fine!" The same applies when a man sees an attractive woman. They each say this because they have beheld the other's beauty. They have seen it, acknowledged it, and they don't have any problem proclaiming the beauty of this person. When a man meets a woman, or a woman meets a man, the first thing they will recognize is the physical beauty. You don't even think about it; it's just automatic. The next thing you know, you're there staring, admiring their beauty.

After you have positioned yourself to come into the presence of God, the next thing you'll need to do is recognize and appreciate His beauty. Men define a woman's beauty by the way her hips are shaped. The way her breasts sit. How pretty her legs are. How gently her hair flows. Women define a man's beauty in sort of the same way. How his butt looks, whether his chest sticks out. How handsome his face is. We define beauty initially not by what the person has on the inside but by what they look like on the outside.

I'm not going to say that it's impossible, but I wager that, nine times out of ten, if you decide to become involved with a man or woman it's not because of their intellect or spirituality. Before you hear what's in that person's heart, you usually notice how they look. Whether or not you fall for the person because of their inward appearance usually follows the fact that you have already noticed and acknowledged their outer beauty. The same applies with God. In order to fall in love with God, you have to recognize and acknowledge His external and internal beauty.

David wrote in Psalm 27:4: *"One thing I have desired of the LORD, that will I seek: that I may dwell in the house of the LORD all the days of my life, to behold the beauty of the LORD, and to inquire in His temple."*

He understood and appreciated God's beauty. He arrived at a place in his life where his eyes became open to see it. David proclaimed that the one thing he desired was to behold the beauty of the Lord. David said this even though he had never beheld all of God's beauty. Like you and I, David could only get a glimpse of God's beauty. We get a glimpse of His inner beauty as we understand more about His love for us. We get a glimpse of His physical beauty as our eyes become open to the beauty of the earth.

Just as a man and a woman have an outward appearance, so does God. However, you can't look at God's legs to see if they are shapely. To check out God's goods, all you need to do is really stop and begin to look around you. When you see the trees you see God. When you see the birds you see God. When you look at the stars at night you're looking at God. If you ever slow down long enough to behold the beauty of God, you won't be able to contain yourself.

If you thought that woman was fine, you should look at God. If you thought that man was fine, you should really take a look at God. God did not create anything that looks better than Himself.

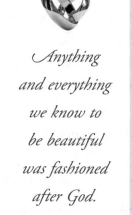

Psalm 50:1–2 (KJV) declares: *"The mighty God, even the LORD, hath spoken, and called the earth from the rising of the sun unto the going down thereof. Out of Zion, the perfection of beauty, God hath shined."*

Anything and everything we know to be beautiful was fashioned after God.

God is described here as the very perfection of beauty, which means God is beauty. Everything that is beautiful is God, and God is everything that is beautiful. Anything and everything we know to be beautiful was fashioned after God. God the Father is the epitome of beauty.

I believe God's greatest testimony of His beauty is found in you and me. Have you ever met someone and they seem to have a glow about them? I've found this to be true with people who are just totally immersed in the goodness of God. They glow with a heavenly glow that is simply beautiful. It seems like their physical attributes are overshadowed by the sure presence of God, which creates a supernatural physical appearance of beauty.

How about the person who was once lost to the world in drug addiction or alcoholism and God comes into their life? Suddenly that which was physically defiled becomes a work of art, as they are spiritually and physically restored through the love of God. It's in those moments you can see the beauty of the Lord in people.

Psalm 96:5–6 (KJV) says: *"For all the gods of the nations are idols: but the LORD made the heavens. Honor and majesty are before him: strength and beauty are in his sanctuary."*

Many human beings have a difficult time recognizing the beauty of God simply because they've been conditioned to know beauty as something completely different. For the most part, we have been conditioned to look for beauty in the things of the world, as opposed to the things of God. A brand-new car looks much better to us than the lilies of the valley. A new house looks much better than the sunrise. We have been groomed to appreciate and chase the things we create, as opposed to the natural creations of God. Subsequently, we "can't see the forest for the trees." To come into a relationship with God requires that we stop looking at the world long enough to notice and then appreciate His natural beauty.

If you are going through a trying time in your life, you're probably at a place where you're slowing down, and you may begin to notice what you've been walking by for so many years.

If life is great and you're reading this, God is still trying to connect with you.

After you meet God and see just how beautiful He is, the next step for you is to go after Him.

Step Three:

Initiate the Inquiry

Once you have beheld the beauty of God you will want to get to know Him better. When a man or woman gets to this point of interest in the opposite sex, they will usually want more information. They usually start by asking questions. I have been in such situations many times. I see a woman who looks good: the first thing I do is ask someone about her. I'll do the very best I can to find out as much as I can about her because I'm putting together a strategy to meet her.

If you are in an office environment you can ask the people you know who are closest to her. They don't have to know her personally, but any information they can give you is going to be helpful. So you inquire whether she has a man in her life. You might ask if she has any children. You ask about her habits. Does she go out to lunch? Does she work late nights? You're trying to find out as much preliminary information as you can.

The details you gather are going to help you decide whether you really want to meet her. If you're not looking for a woman with children and you find out she has one, then she may not be the one for you. If you find a hard working single woman with no children, you may want to move full steam ahead. If you find out she has already been out with five other men in the office, you will probably think twice about even introducing yourself. Whatever the case, the questions you ask of others are going to help you make a major decision.

God is giving you the desire to know more about Him.

The same applies when we finally recognize God and want to get to know Him. You can always know when a person is hungry to meet God. All of a sudden they can't keep their mouth closed about Him. They want to know more. So you'll find them asking questions about God. They ask about His nature, and especially about His history in relationships. They want to know if the things they have heard about Him are true. You will know when and if you are really ready to come into a relationship with God, because you will suddenly be filled with inquiry. You will have all sorts of questions that seemingly come from nowhere.

The fact of the matter is, God is giving you the desire to know more about Him. A beautiful thing happens when people want to know more about God—He will send other people to answer their questions. These people are everywhere. You can find them on the job, in the grocery store, on the playground, and in the church. These are the people who take special pride in telling other people how they came to know God through His Son Jesus Christ. These are the people who will share their testimony on how God brought them out of darkness into light.

Sometimes this inquiry stage can go on for some time, simply because you're about to make the biggest decision of your life, and you want to be sure you're going to invest in someone who is real and able to do all that He says He can. In many cases, when people start asking about God it's because they have already tried everything else, only to come up empty. They want to make sure this decision to seek after God is the right one.

Then there are those people who have been taught everything except the notion of a loving God. They take inquiry to another level. They not only ask questions, they launch an all-out investigative inquiry. The problem is that often these people will spend their time asking questions about God to people who know nothing about Him themselves. As a result, in many cases these people never leave the inquiry stage but, instead, become stuck because of their own doubts and unwillingness to step out in faith.

Then there are those people who will spend no time thinking at all about moving toward God because their lives are so messed up, and they are simply sick and tired of being sick and tired. So after they, too, have tried everything else, they just come running to God. In this case, the inquiry might not last too long.

One thing is sure, the people who want to find out more about God can and will. It takes a combination of the person's desire and willingness, and God's promise that if you look for Him you will find Him.

Matthew 7:7–8 records how Jesus said: *"Ask, and it will be given to you; seek, and you will find; knock, and it will be opened to you. For everyone who asks receives, and he who seeks finds, and to him who knocks it will be opened."*

This is a promise from God, through Jesus Christ, that anyone who seeks out God the Father will find Him. However, it is important to understand that God is really saying, "Keep asking, keep seeking, keep knocking, and one day it will be given, you will find the door will be open."

This is very important, because sometimes we begin to inquire or seek out God and He does not readily appear. It can be like trying to get the prettiest girl or the most handsome guy; you have to work at it for a while. The truth of the matter is, if you give up someone else is going to get them. The only possibility you have of landing that pretty girl or handsome guy is to keep asking about them, keep seeking to get closer, and keep knocking at their door. The moment you stop, you lose.

The same is true when seeking out God Almighty. Sometimes it might appear that He's playing "hard to get." Sometimes it might appear that He is out of reach. Sometimes it might even appear that He is out of your league, but simply remember His promise. If you ask, you will receive. If you seek, you will find. If you knock, the door will be opened to you.

Step Four:

Understand God's Call

Now is a good time to take a step back and try to understand what's going on. So far you have come into contact with this potential new partner. You have been around him or her just long enough to see that they are beautiful. So beautiful, in fact, that you start asking questions of other people who you think might know more about them. You're asking these questions because you have an interest in getting to know this person better.

In the physical world of romance it's all pretty simple. You see someone you're attracted to. You ask questions about them, and you make a move to try to get to know them better. However, in God's spiritual world of romance it doesn't work that way. Entering into a love affair with God is based on spiritual concepts as opposed to the physical and emotional ones experienced with a man or woman. Everything works a little differently with a relationship with God.

Yes, you recognize this new potential partner, God, and, yes, you go as far as to inquire about His nature and how He is in relationships. But if you are experiencing thoughts and feelings about wanting to know God better, they are not coming from you. It was

God who first put them in your head, as it was God who first put the desire in your heart. It was God that turned your head and allowed you to recognize His beauty. It is God who comes after us. God seeks to build relationship with us; we're usually just too busy to ever hear Him.

Even when the circumstances that draw us to Him are painful, it is God's love at the heart of the pain.

In Jeremiah 31:3 we read: *"The Lord has appeared of old to me, saying: 'Yes, I have loved you with an everlasting love; therefore with lovingkindness I have drawn you.'"*

This plainly shows that God calls on us to be in relationship with Him. It even goes as far as to suggest how it is that God calls us: "with lovingkindness." This tells us that it's through God's love that He comes to us and draws us close to Him. We can take refuge in the fact that even when the circumstances that draw us to Him are painful, it is God's love at the heart of the pain. Even if the situations are hard and cause heartache and discomfort, God is at the center watching over us and guiding us through. He guides us through or draws us to Him through those circumstances. It's how God loves us before we ever think about loving Him.

As 1 John 4:19 (KJV) says: *"We love him, because he first loved us."*

This love affair we seek with God is a result of God first loving us to the point that He would beckon us to come to Him.

John 6:64–65 (KJV) reads: *"But there are some of you that believe not. For Jesus knew from the beginning who they were that believed not, and who should betray him. And he said, Therefore said I unto you, that no man can come unto me, except it were given unto him of my Father."*

Jesus wants us to understand that from the beginning He knows who is going to hear God's call and believe in Him. He also makes it very clear in verse 65 that no man can come to Him unless God the Father beckons him. The only way to get to God is through Jesus. The only way to get to Jesus is for God the Father to put that desire in your heart. This invitation to come to God via Jesus Christ is the foundation of Christian theology. Jesus Christ himself offers us the invitation to know the Father by coming through Him.

In Matthew 11:27–29 (KJV), Jesus says: *"All things are delivered unto me of my Father: and no man knoweth the Son, but the Father; neither knoweth any man the Father, save the Son, and he to whomsoever the Son will reveal him. Come unto me, all ye that labour and are heavy laden, and I will give you rest. Take my yoke upon you, and learn of me; for I am meek and lowly in heart: and ye shall find rest unto your souls."*

Note how Jesus says, "Come unto me." That's God's call on our lives. It is an open invitation given to everyone. Some of us never hear it. Others hear it throughout their lives but continue to ignore it until they have no choice but to acknowledge it.

Ever heard of a person who has given their life to the Lord say, "God has been calling me for years"? The fact that they acknowledge

God's call throughout their lives means two things: first, God called and, second, they heard it but decided to ignore it.

One thing is certain, God loves us and continually calls out to us to come to Him. Many of us spend a lifetime and never hear God's call simply because we are too busy with the things of this world. To hear God's call and recognize His beckoning is important. However, the most important thing is our response. Take it from me, when God calls He's going to get your attention one way or the other. Take your pick: will it be the hard way through pain and heartache, or the easy way through your obedience?

God is calling you right now.

Step Five:

Avoid the Haters, the Perpetrators, and the Pleasurenators

The fact that God calls us into a relationship is good news and will mean great things for us—if we do not fall victim to the hater, the perpetrator, or the pleasurenator. While everyone is called by God, very few enter into a relationship with Him. Those who are successful understand that this is the greatest opportunity in life they could ever be given and are willing to protect it.

When you are moving into a new relationship that you feel has potential, you go to great lengths to protect it from negative influences. There are certain people you don't want your new mate around. There are certain places you would not dare take them. You do this all in an effort to shield them from any possible embarrassing situations that could hinder you getting closer. We are particularly careful not to allow our past to get in the way. We make sure the old boyfriend or girlfriend won't pop up and throw a monkey wrench in things.

We do all of this to protect this potentially great new relationship. The same approach is necessary when moving into a relationship with God. Actually, it takes more effort simply because God is

Satan will use everything and everybody to deter you from learning more about God.

the greatest catch you'll ever have. Something that great will come at the greatest sacrifice and effort. Once we have come to a place where we can hear and receive God's invitation to come into a relationship with Him, a war will commence. It will be a spiritual one in which the enemy, Satan, will try to the best of his ability to stop you from forming a relationship with God.

If you thought you had a hard time protecting a new relationship with a man or woman, you haven't seen anything yet. Satan will use everything and everybody to deter you from learning more about God. Knowing this, you must take every precaution to avoid the haters, and not become a perpetrator or a pleasurenator.

A hater is someone who will be used by Satan to try to throw you off course. The spirit of the hater is that of Satan, but can come in the form of the people closest to you. It could mean your mother, father, sister, brother, or even a child is sent on assignment to do or say something to get you to walk away from the things of God and return to the things of Satan. It's important to understand that these people are merely pawns in Satan's game to hurt you. Don't look at them any other way.

You could be the perpetrator if you accept God's invitation but abandon Him and move on when something that you think is better comes along.

Finally, the pleasurenator is the one who receives God's invitation, but the bright lights and action of the world soon lure them back into the same old life of sin.

In summary, some will hear and immediately follow God's call for our lives. Some will hear God's call and begin to follow but decide they would rather stay with their previous partner (Satan). And then there are those who will hear and begin to follow but give up when the relationship gets hard.

Remember that all this happens after God has called you and invited you to come into a relationship with Him. Jesus told us about it in the parable of the sower, in Luke 8:5–15 (KJV):

> *"A sower went out to sow his seed: and as he sowed, some fell by the way side; and it was trodden down, and the fowls of the air devoured it"* (verse 5).

Before we go any further, it's important to know what and who the sower is. A sower of seeds is someone who plants seeds in the ground with hopes that they will spring up and produce fruit, vegetables, or beautiful plants. The sower in this story is a sower of the Word and heart of God. The sower's job is to plant in our minds, hearts, and souls the call of God through His Word. When the sower sows, he is planting God's Word and desire in us. The sower in this scripture is Jesus Himself, who was sent by God to give freely to us the opportunity to get to know Him better, to come into a relationship with Him, to ultimately have a love affair with Him.

Note that the parable begins with the sower going out to sow his seeds. That is yet more reassurance that you can't come after God until God first comes after you. It is also reassurance that He comes after all of us, all the time. But, as I've suggested, different things happen when God comes after us.

Jesus explains things in verses 11 and 12: "*Now the parable is this: The seed is the word of God. Those by the way side are they that hear; then cometh the devil, and taketh away the word out of their hearts, lest they should believe and be saved.*"

This is the hater, Satan, and remember that he could come to you in the form of anyone close to you. This person or situation that arises in your life is there to take away the very Word or invitation God gave you to join Him.

Now let's see what Jesus says about the perpetrator:

> "*And some fell upon a rock; and as soon as it was sprung up, it withered away, because it lacked moisture*" (verse 6).

See what He says about this in verse 13:

> "*Those on the rock are they, which, when they hear, receive the word with joy; and these have no root, which for a while believe, and in time of temptation fall away.*"

These would be the perpetrators. This verse describes the person who accepts God's invitation but does not do the things necessary to build a solid relationship with Him. The seed "withered away, because it lacked moisture." The moisture that is essential for a God-planted seed is constant communication with Him on a personal level, as well as continued fellowship with others who are engaged in a personal relationship with God. That means attaching yourself to a Bible-teaching and -believing church, and being in fellowship with other people who have decided to have a love affair with God. People who do not avail themselves of this kind of discipleship are the ones the Bible says lack spiritual moisture, and eventually they will dry up and die.

Now let's look at the pleasurenators. In verse 7, Jesus says: *"And some fell among thorns; and the thorns sprang up with it, and choked it."*

See what He says about them: *"And that which fell among thorns are they, which, when they have heard, go forth, and are choked with cares and riches and pleasures of this life, and bring no fruit to perfection"* (verse 14). These are the people that hear from God, get excited, and pledge their life to Him. But as soon as a little trial or tribulation comes their way they immediately go back to that which they knew before. In most cases it's the glitter and the gold that attracts them. They want the pleasures of this life, the comforts of living that are usually found in a life of sin.

Finally, we get a glimpse of the character of those who decide to pursue a love relationship with God.

Look at verse 8: *"And other fell on good ground, and sprang up, and bare fruit an hundredfold. And when he had said these things, he cried, he that hath ears to hear, let him hear."*

Now see how Jesus describes them, in verse 15: *"But that on the good ground are they, which in an honest and good heart, having heard the word, keep it, and bring forth fruit with patience."*

These, of course, are the ones who stayed the course and did not allow Satan to influence them to do something outside the will of God. These are the ones who sought an intimate relationship with God. These are the ones who allowed God, through the power of the Holy Spirit, to empower them to experience God the Father in the way He intended.

Because God wants you to be with Him, He does everything to help empower you to make good decisions—choices that will lead you away from the haters, away from the perpetrators, and away from the pleasurenators and right into His arms.

Step Six:

Go for It

If you're able to truly recognize God's call on your life, and assuming you are one of the seeds that fell on good ground, it's time to go to the next step. Isn't it interesting how things change concerning our willingness to take chances once we become attracted to someone? Suddenly we are much more willing to step out and make something happen. It's funny how we create opportunities to come into the same space as the person we're interested in.

They could be on a different street, in a different building, on the opposite side of town, in a different county, in a different state, or maybe even in a different country. It does not really matter how far away they are. If you feel a true yearning, and believe they are the one, you will travel any distance, jump through hoops, and take any chance to engage with your potential new mate.

The effort is to accomplish one thing: to communicate with that person with hopes of getting to know them better. You hope you will discover how great they are and that you will get confirmation that this is, indeed, the person for you. We do all of this naturally. We may be a little nervous and unskilled, but we know that we must somehow come into communication with them.

Sometimes we don't rush in but advance timidly. Usually this is because of fear of rejection or baggage from a previous experience. The baggage in most cases is trust issues and major hurt at the hands of someone else. It's truly amazing how prior relationships with other humans can influence how we move into a relationship with God.

Because of our dealings with people, we have learned that, oftentimes, great excitement and hope can be followed by greater disap-

God wants us to move to Him with reckless abandon.

pointment and despair. Many of us have trusted a man or woman only to be hurt and disappointed. We carry these "soul wounds" around with us for years, while developing a hopeless attitude about relationships. So much so that when a sincere opportunity knocks, our soul wounds activate, releasing negative spiritual, emotional, and mental energy.

The same applies when moving into a personal relationship with God. It should be a no-brainer, but, because of our past, we end up treating God the same as a potential man or woman. We distrust Him even though He's never given us a reason to. We second-guess His call on our lives even though it's the only legitimate invitation of love we've ever received. We doubt His love for us, even though He has given everything in an attempt to prove it.

God wants us to move to Him with reckless abandon. Matter of fact, God does not like that you can go after that man or woman with everything you have, but when it comes to Him you get timid. Not only does God not like it, according to scripture, He is jealous because of it.

When God gave Moses the Ten Commandments, He instructed: *"[F]or you shall worship no other god, for the LORD, whose name is Jealous, is a jealous God"* (Exod. 34:14, emphasis added).

Today we worship all kinds of gods, including the gods of money, fame, power, pride, man, or woman. Anything you have come to love, like, or aspire to more than God Almighty is a god. Your willingness to move into a love relationship with these other gods as opposed to God Almighty kindles jealousy in Him.

Deuteronomy 6:14–15 says: *"You shall not go after other gods, the gods of the peoples who are all around you (for the LORD your God is a jealous God among you), lest the anger of the LORD your God be aroused against you and destroy you from the face of the earth."*

Clearly, it is not good to arouse God's jealousy by your willingness to commit to a person as opposed to Him. Remember, God is calling you into a love affair. He desires to talk to you and allow you to get to know Him better. Religion has given communication with God a bad name. As I have previously observed, most people seem to think they need to change the intonation of their voice and speak in some type of special way when they talk with God.

When we were children our parents did not give us any particular instruction on how to talk to them. Yes, we were taught to speak with respect, but most of what we learned about communicating with our parents came from how we saw them communicate with us. God simply wants you to be yourself. When you talk to your mother or father you come to them and converse as yourself. You don't pretend to be anything else. You wouldn't change the intonation of your voice. You wouldn't speak with any special rhythm. You simply speak in a normal way.

The formal word given to talking with God is prayer. Religion has given it a bad name. Prayer was never meant to be some religious event where ritualistic, meaningless words are spouted off in the direction of the heavens. But sadly that's exactly what it is for most people. We simply imitate what we have heard over the years. The problem is, the people we imitate are simply imitating something they heard from someone else.

There is almost a silent competition among some religious people to see who can rattle off the most religious clichés. This is not a new problem, but it is the main reason people don't have meaningful conversations with God. When Jesus walked the earth, He heard those same sorry, meaningless prayers.

He addressed them this way in Matthew 6:5: *"And when you pray, you shall not be like the hypocrites. For they love to pray standing in the synagogues and on the corners of the streets, that they may be seen by men. Assuredly, I say to you, they have their reward."*

Here Jesus says very plainly to keep it real. Don't spout off a bunch of words that don't mean anything just to make yourself sound like you know how to talk to God. The fact is, the more you use all those words, it demonstrates just how much of a relationship you don't have with God the Father. You're talking loud but saying nothing. Jesus also adds that when you do this you have already received your reward, which is the praise of men.

Then, Jesus goes on to make it very plain how we are to talk to God. In Matthew 6:6–8 He says: *"But you, when you pray, go into your room, and when you have shut your door, pray to your Father who is in the secret place; and your Father who sees in secret will reward you openly. And when you pray, do not use vain repetitions as the heathen do. For they think that they will be heard for their many words. Therefore do not be like them. For your Father knows the things you have need of before you ask Him."*

Jesus is saying to just be yourself and talk to God like you would anyone else. At this point, I need to disagree with every pastor, teacher, or preacher who advises that you need to build a "prayer time" into your life. People in churches all over the world are often encouraged to set aside a particular time of day for prayer. Now, let me be clear: it is important to have special time for you and God. But if you develop a personal relationship with Him, if you enter into a love affair with God, then all times should be special times.

In other words, you should be in continual communication with God. When you are in a relationship with a man or woman, you talk to them whenever you come into their presence. Rarely are we in company with our mate or potential mate and not talking to them. So because God is always with us, we have the opportunity to talk to Him all the time.

When you are in a relationship with someone, you talk to them as much as opportunity permits, but there are times that call for a specific kind of talk.

If you and your mate are in the company of others, your conversation may be limited to general things, like "How was your day?" and "What would you like to eat?" If the two of you happen to be all alone, the conversation could be a lot more personal and even enter an intimate place.

Likewise, though you are in communication with God all day, your conversation will vary depending upon where you are and who is in your company.

When I'm riding in my car talking to God, I'm usually having the type of conversation two friends of the same sex would have. I talk to Him about my likes and dislikes. I ask Him to support me in difficult situations. I laugh at myself with Him about stupid things that I've done. However, if there are some real pressing things going on in my life, I find myself sometimes tearfully crying out to God. I feel very comfortable crying out in the comfort and privacy of my car, even as I am driving down the street.

My conversation with God in public is very different. There I share my sentiments of love and appreciation to Him for all He does for me, but I don't allow other people to hear my personal cries and concerns. Why? Because it's personal and just between God and me.

It's interesting, too, that when we do talk to God we usually don't really expect Him to answer or talk back. Imagine speaking to your biological father. You walk up to him, say what you need to, but then before he can answer you just walk away because you're not expecting him to talk back to you.

That's not likely. When you walk up and say something to them, you stand right there and wait for a response. If you don't get one, you will probably say it again. If you still don't get a response, you might say, "Hey, don't you hear me talking to you?" You do this because you are accustomed to talking to someone and having them respond. Why would you think it would be any different with God?

Yet many of us don't wait for God to talk back. We say what we want to Him, and before He can answer we turn and walk away. Because we never stopped to listen to what God had to say, we assume that He didn't say anything. This could not be further from the truth. The fact is, God spoke but you didn't stay around to hear what He had to say.

Can you imagine talking to the woman or man that you believe is the one for you, only you never give them a chance to respond? Instead of listening to them, you move off thinking that they're not communicating with you, when the real problem is you're moving too fast, never allowing time for them to talk back to you. I don't need to tell you that relationship will be short-lived.

The same applies when communicating with God. You need to talk to God with an expectation that He is going to talk back. It's all about your expectations. If you expect God to show up, God shows up. If you expect God to talk to you, He talks to you.

What you need to understand is the way God chooses to talk to you will be unique and different from the way He talks to anyone else. Remember you are entering a personal relationship. Personal means personal. The way God talks to you will be unique. The way God works through you will be unique. The way God loves you will be unique and personal.

Think about it. Have you ever experienced a relationship where you talk to the other person the exact same way you did someone from your past? A mother with three children will love them all tremendously, but will speak to each of them differently. Though she loves them, in her actions she will love them differently depending on their individual needs. The same applies to our relationship with God. Though He loves us all, depending upon our need He will act differently. When we understand that we can talk to God with the expectation that he will respond, something amazing happens: God talks back!

In Genesis 35:11–13 we read: *"Also God said to him: 'I am God Almighty. Be fruitful and multiply; a nation and a company of nations shall proceed from you, and kings shall come from your body. The land which I gave Abraham and Isaac I give to you; and to your descendants after you I give this land.' Then God went up from him in the place where He talked with him."*

The key thing to notice here is "God said to him." It is very plain: God said to him. In this case it's God talking to Jacob, but it really does not matter. The point is God talked. Verse 13 says that "then God went up from him in the place where He talked with him," indicating again that God, indeed, spoke with Jacob. If God talked to Jacob, then it is within reason to expect that God will talk to us. You need to know that God wants to talk to you. He wants to communicate with you. In the same way you would look for an opportunity to engage with a potential mate, God is looking for the opportunity to engage and talk to you.

There may be times you're talking to God when you feel that He is not listening. What to do then? Well, in a relationship between a man and a woman, when one of them believes the other is not listening, the natural response is to simply talk a little louder, and, in some cases, yell a little.

There are many situations in which you can be tempted to raise your voice. When I used to go to clubs and the party started to jump, everybody in the place would be yelling. When I wanted to be heard I would have to yell a little louder. At a football game everybody may be yelling, but when your team scores you want to be heard, so you will yell a little louder.

We yell loudly about the things that are important to us, the things that we feel strongly about. Sometimes, of course, the things that we think are important aren't really worth yelling loudly about. It wasn't important for me to yell across the street at some woman, "Hey, girl, what's happening?" But I did that kind of silly thing anyway.

Isn't it strange that we will yell about the things we should not, but not the things that we should? If you are a child of God and know that if it were not for His grace you would not know where you'd be, that He has lifted you out of situations that only He could save you from, that it was the blood of Jesus that saved you, you should not mind yelling it out and telling the world that Jesus is your Savior.

Let's look at a man who was not afraid to yell about something that was important to him. We will see that he had something that he needed to say to Jesus and was not going to stop until he did. It's in the story of Jesus and the blind man, told in Luke 18:35–43.

"Then it happened, as He was coming near Jericho, that a certain blind man sat by the road begging. And hearing a multitude passing by, he asked what it meant" (verses 35–36).

A blind man was sitting by the roadside, begging, as Jesus came to Jericho. This man heard the commotion of the crowd that surrounded Jesus as He came down the road. We can learn a lot from this blind man. He knew something was happening. He was not sure what it was, but he knew something was going on. So he stepped up and asked, "What's going on?"

When the time comes for God to show up in your life, you're going to know that something is happening, trust me. When Jesus is about to make His way into your life, you're going to know about it. Something is going to tell you that something is going on.

Look at verse 37: *"So they told him that Jesus of Nazareth was passing by."*

That's a powerful statement. I wonder what people would do these days if they received an email, or saw a newsflash on television, or read in the newspaper that Jesus was passing by? Chances are if I told people right now to get their lives in order, because Jesus is passing by, most would do nothing.

But is it possible that the reason you're reading this book right now is because Jesus is passing by in your life? Is it possible that the time is here, and the time is now—that Jesus is passing by? He's coming down your street. He's coming through your home. He's riding in your car.

Let's see how the blind man in Jericho responded in a similar situation:

> *"And he cried out, saying, 'Jesus, Son of David, have mercy on me!'"* (verse 38).

Notice that he did not call out to Jesus because he saw Him, he called out to Jesus because he had heard that Jesus was there.

This blind man is just like you and me: the only time we ever really fall on our face before God is when we have already fallen down on our face! When we need something beyond what we can do.

Verse 39 continues the account: *"Then those who went before warned him that he should be quiet; but he cried out all the more, 'Son of David, have mercy on me!'"*

When the man cried out for Jesus, the people around him told him to be quiet, to shut up. Don't be surprised as you step out to establish a relationship with God that people will tell you that you're crazy. People will tell you you're calling out for the wrong God.

Now look at verses 40-41: *"So Jesus stood still and commanded him to be brought to Him. And when he had come near, He asked him,* saying, *'What do you want Me to do for you?' He said, 'Lord, that I may receive my sight.'"*

Jesus stood still. That means He must have stopped. When Jesus heard the cry of one in need, He stood still. God wants to have a relationship with you, so when you talk to Him you can be sure He's going to stop to listen to what you have to say.

Look at verse 40 again: *"So Jesus stood still and commanded him to be brought to Him."*

After Jesus stood still, He commanded the blind man be brought to Him. The people were trying to hold the blind man back from entering into a relationship with Jesus, but He commanded them to bring the blind man to Him.

What does this mean for you and me?

There are people who will try to hold us back. There are spiritual demons that will try to hold us back. If we call on the name of Jesus, if we yell "Jesus!" just a little louder, He will stop what He's doing and come. He will demand the people who are holding you back, the demons that are holding you back, turn you lose.

Let's go back to verse 41, and Jesus' response to the blind man: *"'What do you want Me to do for you?' He said, 'Lord, that I may receive my sight.'"*

God loves you. He loves you so much that even right now He'll send Jesus into your spirit to ask you the same question: "What do you want Me to do for you?" God is sitting high and looking low waiting to hear you call on the name of Jesus. Jesus is waiting for the opportunity to come to you and ask you the question, "What do you want me to do?"

The man in this story asked Jesus to restore his eyesight, so let's see how Jesus responded.

Verses 42–43 says:

> "Then Jesus said to him, 'Receive your sight; your faith has made you well.' And immediately he received his sight, and followed Him, glorifying God. And all the people, when they saw it, gave praise to God."

The blind man received his sight by stepping out in faith to connect with Jesus. Once he followed Jesus, Jesus answered his prayer. After Jesus answered his prayer the man glorified God. First he was yelling, "Have mercy on me." Then he was yelling, glorifying God. Like this man, God wants you to yell a little louder. However, you won't have to yell too loud, because God has created a pathway for you to find Him.

You might lack faith in God simply because you have never experienced hearing from Him. If you could actually hear from God you would be more inclined to believe in Him and believe in Jesus. What if you could follow a pathway that could lead you to that place where you could hear from God? Would you want to go there? Would you be willing to do what it takes to go there?

Today, God can lead you to the place where you can hear from Him, to where you can experience Him in ways you never have before. If God is calling you into a deeper understanding of Him, then simply listen to Jesus through the Word of God, and I promise you that if you're willing to go, you will hear from God.

Let's look at another Bible passage, Psalm 95: *"Oh come, let us sing to the LORD! Let us shout joyfully to the Rock of our salvation. Let us come before His presence with thanksgiving; let us shout joyfully to Him with psalms."*

Here we see, as I've stated before, that we come into the presence of God by praising Him for what He has already done in our lives. Next the psalmist tells us why we should sing, why we should shout out to God and praise Him. Verses 3–5 read:

> *"For the LORD is the great God, and the great King above all gods. In His hand are the deep places of the earth; the heights of the hills are His also. The sea is His, for He made it; and His hands formed the dry land."*

So we understand that the first step down the pathway to God is to praise Him for who He is and for what He has already done throughout history. Then, after we have sent up praise to God, we are ready for the next step.

Look at verse 6:

> *"Oh come, let us worship and bow down; let us kneel before the LORD our Maker."*

This tells us we should humble ourselves. The next verse goes on to explain why we should bow down, why we should kneel before

Step Six: Go for It

God Almighty: *"For He is our God, and we are the people of His pasture, and the sheep of His hand. Today, if you will hear His voice."*

The reason we should get on our knees and honor, worship, and praise Him is because He is our God and we are His people.

When the psalmist says "if you will hear His voice," he is not questioning whether God will speak to you. Rather he is questioning whether you will be able to hear God when He does speak—and then, if you hear Him, will you listen?

God wants you to go for it. God wants you to seek Him with all that you have. God wants you to keep seeking, trusting that He can and will show up in your life and show you love in ways that you can't imagine. This is the opportunity of a lifetime. What are you waiting for?

Go for it!

Step Seven:

Understand:
No Faith, No Love

What individual sees the finest man or woman they have ever come in contact with, takes the time to enter their presence, beholds their beauty, but then never goes after them? That's someone you might call a fool. Or, if not a fool, at least someone who does not believe he or she can actually get the prize. For some, no matter how clear the path, they will not step out and take the chance. After all, it is possible that they may be rejected.

That's the main reason some of us don't go after the things we really want in life, isn't it? We are afraid of being turned down, so fearful that we won't even take a chance. When pursuing a love affair with God you don't have to be concerned about rejection. Remember, God says, "If you will seek Me out, you will find Me."

Look at Jesus' words in Matthew 7:7–8: *"Ask, and it will be given to you; seek, and you will find; knock, and it will be opened to you. For everyone who asks receives, and he who seeks finds, and to him who knocks it will be opened."*

Jesus tells us to go after Him with reckless abandon. There is no reason for not giving all that we have to run after a love affair with God. He has already promised that if we seek after Him we will find Him and experience a love affair with Him. God is faithful.

The key to walking in the fullness of God, where you experience the fullness of life, is asking God for the right things. These are the things that God wants us to have. Yes, it's just that simple. When we ask God for the things He already wants us to have, we can be assured that we are going to get them. It's just a matter of time.

What happens when we ask God for what He wants us to have?

Look again at verse 7: *"Ask, and it will be given to you; seek, and you will find; knock, and it will be opened to you."*

According to scripture, when we ask it will be given. If we seek we shall find. If we knock it will be opened to us. This is a guarantee from God. If you're asking for what God wants you to have, it's assured. How do we know this?

Look again at verse 8: *"For everyone who asks receives, and he who seeks finds, and to him who knocks it will be opened."*

It's a guarantee. The problem is we spend a lifetime asking God for things that He is not going to give us simply because they are not what He wants for us. We've got to get in line with what God wants for our lives. Then, and only then, will we have what Psalm 27:13 calls "the goodness of the Lord in the land of the living." God will do that thing for you that is beyond whatever you can imagine.

How can I say this with such confidence? Because He's doing it for me right now.

Step Seven: Understand: No Faith, No Love

Prior to becoming an evangelist, I spent fifteen years in the education field. I started off as a paraprofessional before eventually becoming a teacher. After eight years in the classroom, I felt I'd be more effective as an administrator; that way I'd be a part of the decisions that affected how children would be educated.

Growing up I was a terrible student. By the time I was in high school I had a dual major in basketball and girls. Subsequently, my academic performance left a lot to be desired.

I was the last person in the world any of my teachers, friends, or family would have thought would become an educator. So by the time I received a bachelor's degree in liberal arts, a master's degree in secondary education, and a master's degree in educational administration, I knew I was on the right track. When I became an education administrator I knew that I had found the thing God had put me on the earth to do. I was on the fast track to becoming the next school superintendent. However, that was not to be the case.

I was married at the time, with a child on the way. An administrative salary allowed me to live very comfortably. My then-wife was in social work, and together we were able to live the middle-class American dream. You would think that would be enough for any man, but not so. I started hanging out at the clubs and drinking after work. I'd always been a casual drinker and enjoyed spending time with the boys, but it never interfered with going to work every day and managing my life. One night I decided to smoke marijuana, something that I had done earlier in my life but it hadn't rendered me incapable of functioning. Then one day I decided to try some cocaine. I'd tried that earlier, too, but had not been too fond of it. Only this time I tried smoking it.

From that point on, it was like I was the star of a horror film. One day I was happy, with a wife and child on the way, enjoying the joys of life, then it seemed like only the next day I was walking the streets of Rochester, New York, homeless and looking for the next opportunity to get high.

After many days of suffering, degradation, and humiliation I remembered what my parents had told me when I was young. I remembered their faith in God, and them telling me He would always be there for me. So I called out to this God and I told Him that I needed help. I'd already been through three drug and alcohol rehabilitation programs; I knew I could not stop myself from using. I knew that if God didn't come down and save me, I would die in the streets. So I called out for this God—and nothing happened.

That's right: I'd be on my knees all night long, crying and asking God to save me. The next day I'd get up promising myself that I wouldn't use drugs, and, sure enough, a day or two would go by and I wouldn't use. But, lo and behold, it would be just a matter of time before that demon would call me and, without any control, I would answer. Finally, one day I gave up and yelled out to God: "You promised me that if I called out for you, you'd hear my prayer! Well, if you're not going to come, just let me die." Then, all of a sudden, God showed up. Today I know that He was there all along, but, at that time, I could not see His hand on my life. God picked me up and moved me to another place where He began to pour into me and make me understand why my green pastures had to look and feel the way they did.

I have never picked up another drug since, and today I live every day of my life in service to my Lord and Savior, Jesus Christ. Today, I understand that everything I went through, beginning with my road through the educational world right up through my trials and tribulations with drugs, was all part of God's perfect work in my life and had everything to do with my appointment as an evangelist.

After God delivered me from crack cocaine, He allowed me to grow in ministry and experience several ordained positions, including becoming a pastor. My first call was to be an evangelist, though. God told me that I'd be His evangelist to the nations. Years passed and I began to share God's Word with people in churches and people on the streets, but I still did not see myself as God's evangelist to the nations. But the Word of God says that He can do more than we ask, even more than we can think.

Look at Ephesians 3:20: *"Now to Him who is able to do exceedingly abundantly above all that we ask or think, according to the power that works in us."*

Not only is God faithful, He's faithful to do "exceedingly abundantly above all that we ask or think."

God has been faithful to do exactly what He said He'd do in my life. I've gone on to share the life-changing gospel of Jesus Christ all over this country and internationally. While standing on a stage before tens of thousands of people at a festival in Wisconsin, sharing God's Word, He whispered to me something like, "I told you so. I told you I'd make you an evangelist to the nations." In the midst of my excitement at speaking to so many people that day, I had not recognized that God was doing what He had said He'd do in my life.

God is faithful.

But what exactly is faith? Let's look at how the Bible describes it.

In Hebrews 11:1–3 we read: *"Now faith is the substance of things hoped for, the evidence of things not seen. For by it the elders obtained a good testimony. By faith we understand that the worlds were framed by the word of God, so that the things which are seen were not made of things which are visible."*

The first verse tells us that faith is something that you hope for but cannot see. In short, it's believing in things you can't touch, smell, or see. It's believing in the supernatural. Faith in the Christian

There is a big difference between taking a chance and having faith.

world is believing that Jesus Christ died on the cross, but after spending two days in a grave rose up on that third day. We were not around to see Jesus die or rise from the grave, but as Christians we believe that it happened: that's faith.

Faith is also believing that the same power that allowed Jesus Christ to break the grips of the grave will do the same for us when we die. Yes, we Christians have faith that we will rise from the dead and live eternally with Jesus. That's faith, in the Christian world. In the non-Christian world it's called taking chances. When men and woman enter into a relationship they really don't know each other. They go out on a few dates in an effort to learn more about the other. Truth of the matter is, we go on these dates taking a chance that the person is going to be the type of person we can really learn to appreciate and love.

There is a big difference between taking a chance and having faith, though. When you take a chance you're out there by yourself; whatever goes, goes. On the other hand, when you step out in faith you are, in essence, opening up an opportunity for God to take over your situation. By stepping out in faith you are saying to God that you trust Him and the things you can't see more than you trust yourself and the things that you can see.

Imagine, if you will, God Almighty not showing up in your situation after you have bet the farm on Him. The fact of the matter is He has to show up, or His Word is null and void. However, we have to make sure when we step out in faith that we are actually doing so and not choosing to take another chance. We can ensure ourselves of that by making sure we are following God's lead as opposed to our own.

There is no other way to learn about another person except to take a chance, in hopes that they are right for you. Typically, we will select people to go out with having received no direction from God on the matter. So we step out and take a chance, hoping and believing that it's going to work out. Stepping out in faith is taking a chance, but a very calculated one based on the promises of God.

We seem to have a much easier time trusting and taking chances with men or women than we do God. When starting a relationship with another person there is no great expectation that they have to do certain things for you in order for you to love them. Outside of the woman who expects to be wined and dined, and the man who expects sex for having wined and dined, there is no expectation that the person is going to take care of your every need.

Because of this, we are more tolerant of people when we don't immediately get the things we want. In some cases, we stay in a relationship for years waiting to get from the other person the things that we need and want in our relationship. Sometimes the relationships are even physically or emotionally abusive, but we stay in them hoping for the day things may change.

We are very different with God. When we finally come into a relationship with Him we usually do so because we want and may even need Him to do something for us right away. When we don't get what we want, when we want it, many of us drop God like a bad habit. We may even go as far as to blame Him for our failed situations.

Then there are those who come into a relationship with God having had prayers answered, but as soon as their other requests are not immediately answered by Him they go back to the things of the world they knew prior to coming to Him. Rarely do they ever completely step out in faith believing that God will do what He says He'll do.

Step Seven: Understand: No Faith, No Love

To have a relationship in the Lord we have to have faith. To do a good work in the Lord we also need to have faith. To be all that God has called you to be, the main ingredient is not your work ethic, not your resources, not your eagerness, not your smarts. The key to being successful in your walk in Christ is your ability to allow Him to develop your faith.

There is no way that you can enjoy a love affair with God without faith. No faith, no love. This is true not because I say it, but because God's Word does: *"But without faith it is impossible to please Him, for he who comes to God must believe that He is, and that He is a rewarder of those who diligently seek Him"* (Heb. 11:6).

According to scripture, it is impossible for us to please God without having faith in Him. That means it is impossible for us to be in relationship with Him without faith. Yet even those of us who believe in God can have difficulty having the kind of faith that will sustain a fruitful relationship with Him. As we move toward God we begin to understand that our only chance at true victory in life is through faith in God. In many situations the love affair we want won't come the way we think or when we think, but it will come.

Look at Habakkuk 2:2–4: *"Then the LORD answered me and said: 'Write the vision And make it plain on tablets, that he may run who reads it.' For the vision is yet for an appointed time; but at the end it will speak, and it will not lie. Though it tarries, wait for it; because it will surely come, it will not tarry. 'Behold the proud, his soul is not upright in him; but the just shall live by his faith.'"*

Habakkuk, just like you and me, has been given a message from God—a very plain one. This message comes after Habakkuk questions God, asking why bad things happen to good people. God has just finished explaining to Habakkuk that He is going to allow the Chaldeans, the evil enemy of the Israelites, God's chosen people, to destroy Israel and take them into bondage. Israel has been hardheaded and disobedient. For this, God decides to allow their enemy to come in and whip their behinds.

Habakkuk understands that Israel is hardheaded and disobedient, but he still can't understand why God would allow evil people to destroy these good people. Even though they are hardheaded, they are still good people, he reasons. We, the children of God, are not bad people, but just like the children of Israel we, too, can be hardheaded. If God allowed the wicked to kick the Israelites' behinds, what do you think He will do with us?

God answers Habakkuk by saying He will allow this thing to happen, but it won't last always. He will be there for them.

Look at Habakkuk 2:2–4: *"Then the LORD answered me and said: 'Write the vision and make it plain on tablets, that he may run who reads it.'"*

God wants us to do something. He wanted Habakkuk to write down the vision that He would save Israel. What does God want you to write down? What vision does God want you to accomplish? God wants you to do something simple: allow Him to develop a love relationship with you.

How do you know that, Dexter?

Simple.

God didn't put you down here on earth to do your own thing. He put you down here to do His thing. Remember, God is love and so it only makes perfect sense that He wants you to experience that love, to experience Him.

God speaks to us about the things He wants us to do. One way you can be sure that your ears are open to hearing God's plan for your life is when you stop planning it yourself. As long as you keep making plans to make money and become rich, as long as you keep making plans to become important and popular, and as long as you are controlling your own visions, you won't ever see God's vision for you.

God tells Habakkuk something about the visions and plans that He has given him.

Look at verse 3: *"For the vision is yet for an appointed time; but at the end it will speak, and it will not lie. Though it tarries, wait for it; because it will surely come, it will not tarry."*

God says that the vision that He has given you is for an appointed time. That means that God has already decided when you will see your vision, His plan for your life, come into its fullness. The time has already been established. That means no matter what you do, no matter how hard you work, the time is not going to come until the time comes that God has established. Rest assured, if you are reading this book right now it is a clear indication that God is moving in your life.

Habbakuk is told that "at the end it will speak, and it will not lie." God says, "If I told you something and I told you it will come to pass, then it will." It will not fail, it will not lie. If God said it, it will be.

Then Habbakuk is warned: "Though it tarries, wait for it; Because it will surely come, it will not tarry."

To tarry means to linger or to wait. So this scripture means that though it may be coming slow, wait for it. Though it may not be coming as fast as you would like it to, wait for it. Though it might not be coming the way you want it to, wait for it—because one day it will surely come. That is, if you have faith.

Some of us just can't wait, unfortunately. We get impatient and run off ahead of God. We feel that the relationship should be moving faster than it is, so we decide to try to move it along ourselves.

All this frustration we create for ourselves in vain, because it has already been established when we will move into the things God has prepared. It's kind of like a relationship between a man and woman. One of the two wants to get married right away, but the other is not quite ready. The one who wants it right away will push and push, but their pushing will not make the other person ready.

With God, He is the ready one, waiting for the time when you realize that He is the most important thing in your life. That appointed time has already been established by God. It is an open portal through which you must walk. To do so you must have faith that God will be waiting for you on the other side.

Look at verse 4: *"Behold the proud, his soul is not upright in him; but the just shall live by his faith."*

Habakkuk takes a moment to talk to those people who can't wait for God, those people who don't have faith in what God promises, those people who want to take their lives into their own hands.

Step Seven: Understand: No Faith, No Love

Habakkuk says of them, "His soul is not upright in him." You better "check yourself before you wreck yourself," as the saying goes, because if you are one of those proud people, hell-bent on doing it your way and so proud that no one can tell you anything, the Bible says your very soul is not right.

Verse 4 concludes with a powerful statement: "The just shall live by his faith."

In order to be what God called you to be you must have faith. In order for you to receive heavenly rewards you must have faith. In order for you to rest in the Lord you must have faith. In order to have a love affair with God you must have faith. Without faith, there is no love.

You must also understand that faith is about action. We exercise our faith by what we do. In order to experience a love affair with God, not only must you have faith, you must be willing to put it to work. You must be willing to go after God with everything you have, not knowing exactly what the outcome is going to be, trusting that He will not only see you through it but that He will open a spiritual portal that will allow you to both love and be loved by Him. Faith without works is dead.

James 2:14 says:

"What does it profit, my brethren, if someone says he has faith but does not have works? Can faith save him?"

Now look at verses 15 and 16: *"If a brother or sister is naked and destitute of daily food, and one of you says to them, 'Depart in peace,* be warmed and filled,' but you do not give them the things which are needed for the body, what does it profit?"

These verses clearly demonstrate that having faith without acting on it is of no value. See how it's summed up in verse 17: *"Thus also faith by itself, if it does not have works, is dead."*

Saying that you want a relationship with God without actually taking steps to make it happen will profit you nothing. And know that God is not asking you to do something He has not already done Himself. God has already stepped out and demonstrated His love for you. He has already provided you with enough information to guide your belief system. In the end it's up to you. You have to believe that God can provide the love that you've been missing. You have to believe that a life without the love of God is not a life at all.

Some of us simply don't believe very easily. I for one had to come to believe in the power of God's love. It's been years now since God delivered me from drugs, but I will never forget the process. It included three trips to rehabilitation centers. In actuality, I should have only gone to one because I got the same information each time.

All three times I was told to work the twelve-step program established by Narcotics Anonymous (NA), even though I was a drug addict. I was told to work the same steps as the alcoholic. The first twelve-step fellowship, NA, was founded in 1955 by Bill Wilson and Dr. Bob Smith, known to members as "Bill W." and "Dr. Bob." This program has helped hundreds of thousands of people find sobriety and for many it has also helped them find God.

Step Seven: Understand: No Faith, No Love

The fact that the same steps that can help an alcoholic can help a drug addict tells us that there is something of great value embedded in the twelve steps that can be used to help people with any problem that results in lives of torment, disarray, and even insanity. Your road to a love affair with God is possibly being blocked by torment, disarray, or even insanity. As I have observed, God may use these situations in His effort to move us into a love relationship with Him.

The first two steps of the twelve-step program can be a great help to anyone seeking a love relationship with God. Let's take a closer look at them.

Step one says: "We admitted we were powerless over our addiction, that our lives had become unmanageable."

Before you dismiss the idea that you are an addict, take a moment. The fact is, all of us are addicted to things in this life that move us further away from God. Step one says we finally admit that we are powerless over these things and that, as a result, our lives are not right. Many don't get to the point where their life has become unmanageable, perhaps, but it's pretty bad—maybe so bad, in fact, that you picked up this book with hopes of finding the answer to a better life. That you are reading this means you have some level of faith or belief that God may be the answer.

Step two says: "We came to believe that a Power greater than ourselves could restore us to sanity."

The key phrase here is "came to believe."

It simply implies that even though you may be at a point of belief now, it didn't used to be that way. You did not always believe. And not believing caused you to live a certain way. "Came to believe" implies that after a period of time, experiencing different things in your life, you came to believe something different.

The key is that you came to believe in something greater than yourself. Something more powerful than you. This something has the power to restore you to sanity. This acknowledgment is a huge step, because many of us think we are "all that." Some of us have still not come to believe. Some may think I am overstating things by talking about insanity, but remember the classic definition: doing the same thing over and over again, while expecting different results. You are indeed insane if you are doing the same things in your life, feeling miserable doing them, yet you keep doing them expecting that you'll get a different result.

God wants you to understand that if you are not in Christ Jesus, you are insane. You are sick—sin-sick. This state will lead to only one place, which is death and eternal damnation. The only way to avoid this is to believe in the one being who can restore your sanity, and give you salvation and eternal life: Jesus Christ, the Son of the living God.

All you have to do is have faith and believe that God loves you and is waiting for you to come to Him. Because God wants to be in a relationship with you, be assured that He will be faithful to lead and guide you to Himself. You need only to trust Him and take the leap of faith into His arms.

Step Eight:

Get to Know God Better

After you have spent your time checking out that woman or man and you've finally gotten their attention, you now are running full steam ahead because you think you've found something good. This is the time to stop and spend some significant time trying to get to know that person better. Before you get too serious you need to check them out. Usually, it's all good those first few dates, and you're really feeling good about each other.

This is usually the time, however, when people mess up relationships. Instead of taking time to get to know that man or woman, this is often when you jump into bed with each other. You don't even know who the man or woman really is, but there you are doing all kinds of things.

All you know is that it feels good. Then you wonder why the two of you don't end up staying together. It's because you put the horse before the buggy. You have messed up any opportunity that you may have had with that person. They could have been the right one. Now you'll never know because you have given up the goodies too fast. If you had taken the time to really get to know that person, you could have discovered that this was the right one, or maybe you would have found out that he or she was a devil in disguise.

Having a love relationship with God is very different. First of all, God isn't going to just jump into bed with your dirty behind! God is not going to get intimate with you until He knows that you are ready. So you won't be having any intimate moments with God. The fact is, you can't unless you get to know Him better.

It's very important when entering into a new relationship with someone that you at least know the person's name. Getting to know God better starts with His name. Without going into an in-depth study that would take us away from the direction of this book, you need to know and understand that God has a name. That's right, God has a name just like you and I have names.

If you want to meet a girl or guy, but you don't know their name, there are a couple of things you might try. First, you'd probably ask someone who knows them by name. You might have to dig deeper and research it by asking questions. The same applies with God. If you don't know His name and the significance of it, you might want to ask someone who does know, or better yet research it for yourself.

To help you get started, I'll share God's name with you. It's Yahweh, the name of the Hebrew God. It is represented by the four-letter Hebrew tetragrammatom, which was translated into the Roman script YHWH. In biblical days it was unheard of for anyone to speak God's name. It was considered blasphemous for anyone to utter it. For that reason God's name has been lost, to some degree. If you desire to have a love affair with God it would behoove you to know and understand the origin of His name.

To have a relationship with Yahweh the Father, you must first find His Son, who most of the Christian world knows as Jesus. However, as it is important to know the name of God, it is equally important to know the name of His Son. Again, without going into an in-depth study, His name is Yeshua. This is the proper Hebrew name for Jesus. While He walked the Earth, He was never called Jesus, but Yeshua. It means "salvation," whereas the English version, Jesus, has no meaning. We cannot deny the name Jesus, simply because most of the English-speaking world knows Him by it, but let us establish that the true name of our Savior is Yeshua. This is especially important when you consider the fact that the only way to have a love affair with God is first to embrace His Son Yeshua (Jesus).

In John 14:6, Jesus says to Thomas after the resurrection: "*I am the way, the truth, and the life. No one comes to the Father except through Me.*"

According to scripture, the only way we can have a relationship of any kind with Yahweh is to first go through Yeshua. So it is in that spirit that Yeshua beckons us to come unto Him, to come to the Father. Yeshua understands that the only way we can really have peace, the only way we can really experience joy, the only way we can really live out the vision that God has for our lives, the only way to have a love affair with God, is if we come to Him, to be in fellowship with Him and really get to know Him better.

Look at Matthew 11:28: *"Come to Me, all you who labor and are heavy laden, and I will give you rest."*

Yeshua tells us to come unto Him. Then He is specific about who it is that He is calling—it is all who labor and are heavy laden. Labor means you are working. Laden means you are weighed down or burdened. Yeshua even goes as far to say heavy laden—weighed down a lot. When we put the two conditions together what we can understand is that Yeshua is saying, "If you are working, but the work you're doing is heavy and you are burdened by all you have to do, come to Me."

It is important to understand that Yeshua is not talking to people who are burdened by what they do on their jobs. Rather, He is talking to people who are engaged in working out their soul salvation. He is talking to those of us who are seeking a relationship

If you want to know Him better you need to spend some time with Him.

with the Father, but for whom it seems hard and heavy, so heavy that, at times, we just want to walk away from it. If you are feeling that way, Yeshua is saying to you, "Come to Me and I will give you rest. I will show you how to come into relationship with God."

Many people are experiencing emptiness in their lives. It seems like no matter what they do, or how much they accomplish in life, they still have an empty, incomplete feeling. If this is you, Yeshua is saying, "Come to Me, and I'll take care of that for you."

Look at verses 29 and 30: *Take My yoke upon you and learn from Me, for I am gentle and lowly in heart, and you will find rest for your souls. For My yoke is easy and My burden is light.*

When Yeshua says to take His yoke upon you, He is calling you into a closer and deeper relationship with Him, so that you can come into a deeper and closer relationship with the Father. The word "yoke" means bondage or a burden. Yeshua tells us to take on His yoke as opposed to the yoke of the world. Take on His yoke because it is easy. The burden that He will put on you is light. By doing this, Yeshua says, you will find rest for your soul.

Yeshua says that if you want to know Him better you need to spend some time with Him. And He wants to spend time with you. "By getting to know Me better," He is saying, "I will introduce you to the love and compassion of the Father, of Daddy, of Poppa, of Yahweh, of Elohim, of Adonai, or as most of you know Him, God Almighty." Yeshua says, "I'm not going to put more on you than you can bear. You will have peace while you walk with Me."

Yeshua desires to be in relationship with you: that's why you were born. You were born to be in relationship with Yahweh the Father, with Yeshua the Son, and the Holy Spirit. We were born to be connected to them. They are three personalities but they are one, and they want to be in fellowship with you. Your soul knows it, so your soul reaches out for it. Your soul cries out for it. Just know that it is the intention of Yeshua for us to be one with Him and the Father.

Look at John 17:20: *"I do not pray for these alone, but also for those who will believe in Me through their word."*

Yeshua has just finished praying for His twelve disciples. Now He is praying for those people who will believe in Him through the words of His disciples. He's praying for you and me.

Now look at verse 21, where He prays that *"they all may be one, as You, Father, are in Me, and I in You; that they also may be one in Us, that the world may believe that You sent Me."*

Yeshua is praying that you and I would be in Him and in God as they are inside of one another. He is praying that you and I will be connected to them. Yeshua is praying that you and I be in a relationship with them.

In verse 22 Jesus goes on: *"And the glory which You gave Me I have given them, that they may be one just as We are one."*

What glory is Yeshua talking about? What has He given to us so that we may be one just as they are one? God gave Yeshua the Spirit of truth, the Holy Spirit. Yeshua is saying that the same Spirit that He used to be one with God is the same one that He gave us that we, too, may be one with God. That we may be connected to the Father in the same way that He is. That we may have a love affair with God.

Look at Jesus' desire, as He expresses it in verse 23:

"I in them, and You in Me; that they may be made perfect in one, and that the world may know that You have sent Me, and have loved them as You have loved Me."

Step Eight: Get to Know God Better

When we come into relationship with Yeshua, when we come into relationship with the Father, then, and only then, can we experience perfection as we are one with the Father, and the Son, and the Holy Spirit.

Yahweh wants us to get away from "having church" and instead become "the church." The Father is not interested in how well we have service on Sunday. He is more concerned about our relationship with Him Monday through Sunday. Yeshua is not impressed by the way we sing, dance, shout, and praise if we do those things when we don't have a relationship with Him.

There will be many people on Judgment Day that will be crying, "Lord, didn't you like the way I sang your praises? Didn't you like the way I prayed those prayers? Didn't you like the way I preached those sermons?" God wants you to know that a lot of people are going to die and go to hell because they have never taken the time to get to know Yeshua and they have never taken the time to get to know the Father. To those people Jesus says, "I will not know them."

Don't believe me? Read it for yourself in Matthew 7:21: *"Not everyone who says to Me, 'Lord, Lord,' shall enter the kingdom of heaven, but he who does the will of My Father in heaven."*

According to Jesus not all who say "Lord, Lord" will be saved. Why? Because they have not done the Father's will. So here's a question for you: How can you do the Father's will if you have never taken time to get to know Him? The answer is you can't. You can't please God if you don't know Him. And you can't know Him unless you know Yeshua.

Look at verse 22: *"Many will say to Me in that day, 'Lord, Lord, have we not prophesied in Your name, cast out demons in Your name, and done many wonders in Your name?'"*

These are the workers I was telling you about. They are the people who are busy doing the work in the church but not being the church. These are the people who will be crying out "Lord, Lord" because they never took the time to get to know Him better.

Look at verse 23: *"And then I will declare to them, 'I never knew you; depart from Me, you who practice lawlessness!'"*

"I never knew you! I never knew you!" That is a scary thought. But it does not have to be that way.

Through His Son, Yeshua, we get the opportunity to begin a real relationship with God the Father. As we allow Christ to bring us closer to God, we begin to understand who God is. If you spend some time getting to know God you will come to understand that He is love. If you hang around God you will know love. To know love is to know God, because God is love.

Look at 1 John 4:8–9: *"He who does not love does not know God, for God is love."*

According to scripture, God is love. So now we only need to understand what love is and we'll get a great understanding about God.

Look at 1 Corinthians 13:4–7: *"Love suffers long and is kind; love does not envy; love does not parade itself, is not puffed up; does not behave rudely, does not seek its own, is not provoked, thinks no evil;*

does not rejoice in iniquity, but rejoices in the truth; bears all things, believes all things, hopes all things, endures all things."

To bring this into perspective we need only replace the word "love" with "God." Now it reads like this:

> God suffers long and is kind;
> God does not envy;
> God does not parade Himself, is not puffed up;
> God does not behave rudely, does not seek His own, is not
>   provoked, thinks no evil;
> God does not rejoice in iniquity, but rejoices in the truth;
>   God bears all things, believes all things, hopes all things,
>   endures all things.

When you begin to come into the knowledge of Yahweh, you understand that He is everything you've ever thought that is good. He is the very essence of everything perfect. He is the greatest feeling you can imagine. He is love. To understand this concept better we need to become familiar with the things that are encompassed by God's love.

According to Galatians 5:22–23: *"But the fruit of the Spirit is love, joy, peace, longsuffering, kindness, goodness, faithfulness, gentleness, self-control. Against such there is no law."*

In a new relationship, a man and a woman will introduce themselves to the other. Customarily, they each describe themselves as the kind of person they believe they are. If God were to introduce Himself to you, it might sound something like this:

Hi,

I am Love. You can easily recognize Me because I'm always caring for someone. I try very hard to find the good in everyone, and I always accept people for who they are, and love them for who they are. I am love.

I am Joy. I'm easy to spot because there is always delight and enjoyment happening all around Me. I am the very source of happiness. I am Joy.

I am Peace. You can always tell when I'm around because there is harmony all around Me. I represent the cool, quiet, calm place in your life. I am Peace.

I am Forgiveness. I pride Myself on being patient with others and providing them with opportunities to correct their wrongs. I am merciful and tolerant, full of understanding. I am Forgiveness.

I am Kindness. You know Me: I am the thoughtful One. I'm the helpful One. My every thought is full of compassion and sympathy for others. I am Kindness.

I am Goodness, first cousin to Kindness. We're very much alike. I am, however, the most decent being you'll ever meet. Honesty is the core of My soul, and righteousness My divine guide. I am Goodness.

I am Faithful. I'm the One you can depend on. My closest friends call Me trustworthy. I am dependable and devoted. Loyalty and commitment sum up the nature of My character. I am Faithful.

I am Gentleness. I am adored by many for My mild, calm, peaceful nature. I am kind; I never use excessive force to accomplish My goals. I'm meek, I'm mild. I am Gentleness.

Step Eight: Get to Know God Better

I am Self-control. I possess great willpower. No one—and I mean no one—can push My buttons. I am disciplined and always in full control of My actions. I am Self-control.

I am the great I Am. I am the One and only true living God, responsible for forming the heavens and the earth, responsible for the creation of the birds and the trees, responsible for the creation of humanity. I am the author of love, mercy, and grace. I am the God who gave you the Savior named Yeshua.

I am Yahweh, the One and only true and living God.

Now we know more about who God is, we understand that He is a loving God, a kind God, and a long-suffering God. God believes all things, He bears all things, He hopes all things, and He endures all things—not some things, but all things. We know from Galatians 5:22–23 that God is a God of *"love, joy, peace, long-suffering, kindness, goodness, faithfulness, gentleness and self-control."*

I don't know about you, but if I ran into a woman who had a character like this, I'd be ready to spend my life with her. I would understand that she was precious and special. There would be nothing in the world to stop me from trying to spend the rest of my life with her.

Now I'm ready to marry God.

Step Nine:

Get Intimate

We were all created for intimacy with God. Some reading that statement may be somewhat offended at the notion of being intimate with God. When we hear the word "intimacy," immediately our flesh comes alive and we begin to think of intimate encounters we may have had with men or women. So we try to incorporate and compare these kinds of intimate encounters with the thought of an intimate encounter with God. Because our minds can't understand or accept the possibility, we simply reject it. We convince ourselves that it's dirty, nasty, or disrespectful to think of God in that light.

The reason for this is that most of us have never really experienced true intimacy. To do so we would have had an encounter with another person in which each person was totally unselfish, wanting and needing only to bring joy, happiness, and pleasure to the other person, while not expecting anything in return. To really be intimate with another person requires that one gives totally of oneself. In today's society, you would be hard-pressed to find two individuals willing to give in that manner.

Because we have really never experienced true intimacy, we don't really know what it is or what it feels like. If you ask the average person to describe an intimate encounter, they will probably describe a sexual experience. More to the point, they will probably describe one that they considered satisfying and rewarding. Intimacy for most of us is no more than a good sexual experience.

But true intimacy does not have anything to do with a sexual experience. The real definition of intimacy is closeness, friendship, warmth, or comfort. Having an intimate relationship with God simply means you are now completely open to experience Him, to grow close to Him, to know Him in a personal way. It's through an intimate encounter with God that you'll be able to fully discover and experience His unconditional love.

To know what love is, you may have to first discover what it's not; so it is with intimacy. We spend years of our lives trying to find that right person to enjoy an intimate relationship with. If we are smart, we allow God to give us that person and our hunt is short-lived. If we are not connected to God, that hunt can go on for years as we experience man after man, woman after woman, all to find that one person with whom we can be truly intimate.

After we think we've found that special one, many of us will discover that there is still something missing. It's at that point that many married people fall into adultery. They do so because they are still unfulfilled. There is something missing that they thought they would be receiving through their sexual relationship with their mate. Time has now revealed that they were just experiencing a temporary fix. Their innermost being is still looking and searching for that fulfilling relationship.

For the married person, now they are engaging in adulterous behavior and moving further away from God. For the unmarried person, they are still moving from year to year, man to man, woman to woman, and bed to bed. The truth of the matter is that the intimate experience we thought we had with that particular person, the one that felt right at first, later proved to be wrong. It was, in actuality, just another sexual experience.

God wants us to enjoy an intimate experience with Him as a part of our love affair with Him. God desires intimacy with us and, whether we recognize it or not, we desire intimacy with Him. It is that innermost feeling that each of us has. It's our very soul crying out for the relationship with God that He intended from the beginning when He created man and woman in His own image. Not only that, but God also created everything in the earth and all that comes from it.

Isaiah 42:5 says: *"Thus says God the LORD, who created the heavens and stretched them out, who spread forth the earth and that which comes from it, who gives breath to the people on it, and spirit to those who walk on it."*

God created the heavens and earth and that which comes from it, including love and intimacy, emotions and feelings. God created the notion of intimacy, laughter, joy, and happiness, as well as pain, suffering, trials, and tribulations. God created it all. He created it all that we might experience it, but in a godly way. God's intention is to draw us near to Him. We draw near to God by seeking Him out and submitting our lives to Him.

James 4:7–8: *"Therefore submit to God. Resist the devil and he will flee from you. Draw near to God and He will draw near to you. Cleanse your hands, you sinners; and purify your hearts, you double-minded."*

The only way to experience true intimacy is to give all of yourself to a relationship.

The book of James admonishes us to submit to God, to surrender our lives to Him. It goes on to say that we should draw near to God, promising that He will in turn draw near to us. God is closer than you think: you need only call out and be ready to humbly surrender to Him. The only way to experience true intimacy is to give all of yourself to a relationship; to have intimacy with God you have to be able to open up and give all of you to Him. That is true surrender.

Have you ever had to surrender the license plates to your car? Did you give the authorities half a plate? A person surrendering themselves to the police, do they surrender half of themselves? To surrender you must give all. So many of us have been in relationships where we expected great things but never really gave all of ourselves. You can't expect to receive all if you're not willing to give all. To truly experience intimacy with God you must totally surrender to Him.

Step Nine: Get Intimate

Job 22:21–22 says: *"Now acquaint yourself with Him, and be at peace; thereby good will come to you. Receive, please, instruction from His mouth, and lay up His words in your heart."*

The scripture instructs us to acquaint ourselves with God, and nothing but good will come to us.

Now, look at what comes next in verse 23: *"If you return to the Almighty, you will be built up; you will remove iniquity far from your tents."*

You may be wondering, what does "return to the Lord" mean? God's original intent was that we should know Him intimately as Adam and Eve did before the fall, but that relationship was severed by sin. Remember, I wrote earlier that before we were physically born, we were in a perfect relationship with God. Once we were born to this world, we became sinners and were disconnected from Him. The scripture tells us to return to the Almighty and be empowered by the Holy Spirit.

Look at verse 24: *"Then you will lay your gold in the dust, and the gold of Ophir among the stones of the brooks."*

When we come back to God, He empowers us to say no to the things of the world. The scripture says, "Then you will lay your gold in the dust," which means we will be able to put God first. When you decide to surrender all to God you'll put away your love for money, riches, power, and control.

Look at verse 25: *"Yes, the Almighty will be your gold and your precious silver."*

A true indication of surrender is our willingness to sacrifice our material wealth and the things of the world to have a relationship with God. This scripture suggests that our love for God should replace the love we have for the things of the world.

Look at verse 26: *"For then you will have your delight in the Almighty, and lift up your face to God."*

According to scripture, once you have made God the most important thing in your life, then and only then can you truly dedicate yourself to Him. In other words, as long as there are other things that are more important to you than God, you'll never be able to enjoy intimacy with Him. He's not going to settle for being second to anything or anyone in your life. Once you give all to Him, He will give all to you.

Don't believe me? Read it for yourself in verses 27–28: *"You will make your prayer to Him, He will hear you, and you will pay your vows. You will also declare a thing, and it will be established for you; so light will shine on your ways."*

When you decide to commit to God, the Bible says that you will pray to Him and He will hear you. You will ask of Him and He will make it happen, and you will be the light of the world. This is available for anyone who will trust in God and step out in faith. God is just sitting there waiting for you to come. He's so close to you right now.

Psalm 145:18–19: *"The LORD is near to all who call upon Him, to all who call upon Him in truth. He will fulfill the desire of those who fear Him; He also will hear their cry and save them."*

Step Nine: Get Intimate

This leaves little to the imagination. Clearly, God is near to anyone who wants to be near to Him. It also promises that He will answer the call of anyone who calls out to Him in sincerity. The real question is, do you want to draw near to God? I mean, do you really want a love affair with Him? How badly do you really want it?

Automatically a question should arise from that question: how badly do we want what? So that there is no confusion, if I spell out the entire question it would read: how badly do you want a love affair with God? Under that question would also follow a series of smaller questions. Just how badly do you want the marriage of salvation? How badly do you want intimacy with Him?

In the Christian world, you'll never have any problem finding people who say they want a relationship with God. Most would say that is the very reason they gave their life to God. Most will say that they are "in it to win it," that they are there for the duration. You will find many women and men who say they are sold out to God, yet when the strong winds of life's difficulties blow, they give up.

Some that fall are able to get back up.

Look closer and you will find that not everyone who says they are in it to win it, really is. To really be in it to win it, you've got to want it really bad. A love affair with God has to be the most important thing in your life. That means nothing, and I mean nothing, comes before it.

Let's take a moment and look at a woman who wanted intimacy really bad, a woman who would stop at nothing to have her life be touched and changed by God in an intimate way.

Luke 8:43–44 tells us: *"Now a woman, having a flow of blood for twelve years, who had spent all her livelihood on physicians and could not be healed by any, came from behind and touched the border of His garment. And immediately her flow of blood stopped."*

The Bible reports that a woman who had been bleeding for twelve years had spent all of her money going to doctors, but none could heal her. So the Bible tells us that this woman came through a multitude of people and touched the garment that Jesus was wearing.

Notice that the crowd thronged Him; that means they were pushing against Jesus. Everyone wanted to get next to Jesus, so there were many people touching Him.

Somehow this woman pushed through every man in the crowd. She pushed past every woman and child in the crowd. She pushed through a multitude of people so that she could touch Jesus. This woman must have realized that it was a long shot for her to get an opportunity to touch Him.

Touching someone is highly intimate. You can't just walk up and touch people. She knew that she could not just walk up to Jesus and ask for what she wanted. She couldn't come through the front door, so the Bible tells us how she went through the back door looking for a chance to touch Him.

Verse 44 says that she *"came from behind and touched the border of His garment. And immediately her flow of blood stopped."*

She had been sick for twelve years, spending all her money seeking help. She could have given up during the first or the second year of her illness. She could have just accepted that she was always going to be bleeding. She could have given up, but she didn't. She kept on searching until one day she ran into a man named Jesus. And when she touched Him, she was made well.

This woman desperately wanted to see Jesus. She was not going to stop until she got her blessing. She was willing to do anything, even break the law and maybe risk her life, for the one opportunity to have this intimate encounter with Him.

No doubt she was a woman who had been kicked to the curb by society. I've heard comments from my wife about the pain and agony associated with a woman's monthly cycle; imagine dealing with that constantly for twelve years.

But this day was a special day. This woman had heard about a man named Jesus. She had heard that He could give sight to the blind. She had heard that He made the lame walk and the mute talk. She had heard that this man Jesus could make everything all right. She needed Him. She wanted an intimate relationship with Him. There was nothing more important to her this day than getting to Him. He was her only hope, her only chance at living a life that was pleasing to God. Without Him she was going to remain dirty, defiled, and unclean all the days of her life.

Some of us could learn from our sister with the issue of blood.

How badly do you want to be healed of your sickness? Jesus says, "Well, if you want Me to heal you, believe in Me. Believe that I am capable of doing anything. Have faith in Me and ask and you shall receive."

How badly do you want to be delivered from the strongholds of drugs, alcohol, lying, or cheating? "Well, if you really want deliverance," Jesus says, "ask Me for it, then count it as done. Whether it looks that way to you, it has already been done. Believe it and you will receive it!"

The woman with an issue of blood wanted it more than anything. She was willing to risk everything to be with Jesus. What happens when we are ready to abandon everything and pursue God with all of our heart, with all of our mind, and with all of our soul? How will God respond to us when we fight through crowds to get to Him, when we wake early in the morning seeking Him, when we don't allow anything or anybody to come before Him? How will God respond to us? Let's see.

The narrative continues in Luke 8:45: *"And Jesus said, 'Who touched Me?' When all denied it, Peter and those with him said, 'Master, the multitudes throng and press You, and You say, "Who touched Me?"*

The first thing that God wants you to know is that when you begin to push through the crowd to meet Him, when you step out and search for Him and reach out for Him, when you reach out and touch Him, He will notice you.

Jesus asked who touched Him. He knew that this woman was seeking Him. He knew that there was somebody in the crowd who was willing to know Him at all costs. When you touch Him, no matter what's going on with Him, He's going to stop and acknowledge you.

I don't know about you, but that's good news for me.

Now look at verse 46: *"But Jesus said, 'Somebody touched Me, for I perceived power going out from Me.'"*

The next thing you can shout about is that when you reach out and touch Him, He will release His power into you. This account reads like Jesus can't help but give you power when you seek Him. It's a part of His nature to bless you. The verse records that Jesus perceived power going out from Him. He will release His healing, deliverance, and love power into your life—that is, if you want it.

Look at verse 47: *"Now when the woman saw that she was not hidden, she came trembling; and falling down before Him, she declared to Him in the presence of all the people the reason she had touched Him and how she was healed immediately."*

This woman had to "fess up." She had to tell all the people around her and tell Jesus that she had done this thing. More importantly, she got an opportunity to tell the world that she was sick, but since she touched Jesus she was healed. She gave the world her testimony of the saving, healing, and delivering power of Jesus Christ. As she spoke, she was afraid and trembling.

When she was done, verse 48 says, Jesus told her: *"Daughter, be of good cheer; your faith has made you well. Go in peace."*

To seek Jesus with all your heart, mind, body, and soul you must first have faith. For having that faith Jesus will reward you and bless you. God created intimacy to be experienced with Him. It should be a beautiful, godly experience, but we have allowed Satan to cheapen it for us in a very dirty, nasty, disrespectful way. God's intention was for us to experience Him in a very intimate, personal, and loving way. We have moved far from this notion and continue to suffer the results associated with the separation of a child from a loving father. But God still waits for us to call upon Him.

Jeremiah 33:3 says: *"Call to Me, and I will answer you, and show you great and mighty things, which you do not know."*

Step Ten:
The Marriage Ceremony

At this point in a relationship, you know that this man or woman is the best thing that has ever happened to you. You also understand that to make your relationship pure and holy you must be willing to marry him or her. To go to the next step of intimacy, you must first be ready to make a commitment. A permanent commitment. A lasting commitment. A "'til-death-do-us-part" commitment.

The same applies when you are seeking a love affair with God. You must be ready to make a lifetime commitment to God—but remember that this commitment has to come through His Son, Yeshua.

Romans 10:8–9 says: *"But what does it say? 'The word is near you, in your mouth and in your heart (that is, the word of faith which we preach): that if you confess with your mouth the Lord Jesus and believe in your heart that God has raised Him from the dead, you will be saved.'"*

Salvation is the key to a permanent commitment to God. Salvation, simply put, is the result of your declaration before man and God that you believe in God's Son, Yeshua. It is a declaration that you believe that Yeshua is God Almighty Himself come down to the earth as a man. It's a belief that Yeshua walked the earth providing humanity the one example of perfection, the one example of what it looks like to live a sinless life. And it is the belief that Yeshua was crucified for our sins and rose from the grave after three days.

In a traditional marriage ceremony, the man and woman are asked to repeat certain vows. Most of us have heard some of them before: for richer or poorer, for better or worse, in sickness and in health, until death do us part. Similar to the vows a man and woman make to each other, there is an audible confession of faith we have to make to God Almighty. This confession of faith simply says, "I believe, and I want to be in a relationship with God."

Romans 10:9 reminds us that two things are necessary to come into a relationship with God, "*that if you confess with your mouth the Lord Jesus and believe in your heart that God has raised Him from the dead, you will be saved.*"

According to scripture, it is necessary to both confess our belief with our mouth and believe it in our heart. It makes sense, right? What man would tell a woman he loved her if he did not first believe it in his heart? Never mind—don't answer that! However, the point is we have to make a proclamation to God if we want to have a love affair with Him. This proclamation is very similar to the one you might witness at a marriage ceremony.

When you walk down the aisle with that man or woman, you will have to make a commitment to them, publicly announcing that you are committing your life to them for as long as you live. The same applies with God. To have a love affair with God, you have to commit to Him for the rest of your life. You have to stand before man and God and say that you believe in Jesus. You believe He died on the cross and rose after three days, with all power in His hands.

This commitment to God is a commitment to the end.

"Til death do us part" is a familiar phrase. Anyone who has witnessed a man and a woman being joined in holy matrimony has heard these words. During the wedding ceremony, both the man and the woman agree that once they are pronounced a couple under no circumstances should they ever be separated. The two agree that the only way they will be separated is by death, meaning that one of them would have to die. That's 'til death do they part.

However, let's look at that phrase in a bit of a different light.

When we are born each of us forms a relationship with the world. We are born into a certain lifestyle. Most of us grow up learning and trying to accomplish what the world tells us is important. For example, that it's important to go to school and graduate. So everybody endeavors to do that. The world also tells us to go to college after high school and, afterward, to seek a good job. So most of us at least try to do that.

The world also tells us when to go to our first party, when to take our first drink, when to have that first boyfriend or girlfriend, and when to have sex. The world tells us the right age and the right times to do all those things. We grow up chasing the American dream: money, houses, cars, power, control. We chase after these things because the world tells us that's what we're supposed to do.

The only way to live with God, to marry God, is to die to the world.

Some of us will chase these things all of our life, then die and go to hell. Some of us are fortunate enough, blessed enough, to get a message from God telling us that these things we've been chasing are the very things that will lead us to hell. Some of us are blessed enough that God will step into our lives and say, "Enough is enough is enough. Now is the time that you stop chasing after the world and start storing up some treasures in heaven."

When this happens, we are faced with a decision: either we can live for the world or die for the Lord. That's right, we are faced with a major decision to live or to die. God makes us understand that we can't have both Him and the world. So the relationship that we came into when we were born into this world needs to end. The only way for that "marriage" to end is by death: "'til death do us part." The only way to live with God, to marry God, is to die to the world.

Take a look at John 12:23: *"But Jesus answered them, saying, 'The hour has come that the Son of Man should be glorified.'"*

To bring you up to speed, here we are joining Jesus at the end of His earthly ministry. He's done many miracles. He's preached about the Kingdom of God, and the time is near when He must die for the sins of this world.

Look at verse 24: *"Most assuredly, I say to you, unless a grain of wheat falls into the ground and dies, it remains alone; but if it dies, it produces much grain."*

Jesus speaks to His disciples in classic style, telling them a scientific fact to make them understand a spiritual truth. Allow me to make it plain: Jesus says that unless the seed that goes into the ground dies, it can't reproduce. This is a scientific fact. When a seed goes in the ground it has to change, or die, from the form that is sown in order for another form to come out of the ground.

If the seed that goes in the ground dies, then it can become alive again, taking on a different body, and this new body produces much. If you look at the root of a plant that has sprouted, you'll find that at the root is the seed you put in the ground, but you won't recognize it because it has changed into something else. The something else is a plant that produces more of whatever it is. If it was an orange seed before it died, it will produce many oranges. If it was an apple seed it will produce lots of apples.

What is Jesus trying to tell us? Right after He says, "The hour has come that the Son of Man should be glorified," Jesus tells us the story of the dying seed. He tells the story of Himself. Jesus is saying, "I am the seed of life. I'm a good seed all by myself, but if I die, more good seeds will come forth." Jesus is telling us why He has to die. Jesus must die in order for you and me to be born. Not born physically, but Jesus must die in order for you and I to be born again. Like the apple seed that has to die to produce more apples, the seed-Jesus had to die to produce more brothers and sisters like Him.

After making that plain, Jesus goes on to explain the philosophy behind receiving eternal life. In verse 25 He says:

> *"He who loves his life will lose it, and he who hates his life in this world will keep it for eternal life."*

Somehow our spirits must have an idea of how good Adam and Eve had it. Why do I say that? Because we spend all our lives trying to recreate the peace that they enjoyed before God required them to leave the Garden of Eden. We try to make life comfortable by buying things, trying to feel good and have fun, enjoying all the pleasures of life. It's part of our nature to want to enjoy the world. That's the way we're born. We're born crying for Momma to feed us, rock us, comfort us. We spend our lives trying to get that feel-good thing.

Then, Jesus comes along and blows it for everybody! He says that if you love the life of the world, you will lose your life. If you hate the life of the world, then you will keep life forever. The problem is too many of us like the feel-good experience of the world. Many of us like it so much that we're not ready to trade it in for a God we can't see. So we simply try to have both: I'll have a piece of God, and I'll have a piece of the world, please.

God says, "Actually, no you won't." Either you can live for the world, die, and go to hell, or you can die to the world and live eternally with Him.

Look at verse 26:

"If anyone serves Me, let him follow Me; and where I am, there My servant will be also. If anyone serves Me, him My Father will honor."

Jesus says that if you want to serve Him, if you want to be with Him, then follow Him. In other words, do exactly what He does. Some people get happy about the idea of following Jesus and stay that way until they understand what Jesus meant here. You see, Jesus is talking about how He is about to die. Jesus is saying, "If you want to be with Me, if you want to serve Me, if you love Me, come do what I'm about to do. I'm about to die for brothers and sisters I don't even know. I'm about to let them whip me and kill Me. If you love Me, you'll do the same."

That's when we stop being happy about following Jesus! We'll follow Jesus anywhere, as long as it does not require us to suffer or to sacrifice our time, talents, or money. When you start talking about pain and suffering and sacrificing, all of a sudden we're often not so interested in serving Jesus.

Look at verse 27: *"Now My soul is troubled, and what shall I say? 'Father, save Me from this hour'? But for this purpose I came to this hour."*

Jesus already knew that when it came time for us to die to the sins of this world we would have trouble. He knew when it came time for us to stand up before this world and profess and confess Jesus Christ as Lord, we were going to have problems doing it. This is why I love Jesus so much: He always goes through the difficult things for us first. He does not send us to do something He Himself did not do. So, in this verse Jesus says, *"Now My soul is troubled, and what shall I say?"*

Jesus is thinking about His crucifixion. He's thinking about the pain He's about to endure. He's thinking about the suffering He's about to experience. "I'm having a hard time dealing with this," He says. "I know I must do it, but it's hard." Be sure about this: if it was hard for Jesus to die for the sin of the world, it's going to be hard for you to die to the sins of the world. But look again at what Jesus says in that same verse:

> *"Now My soul is troubled, and what shall I say? 'Father, save Me from this hour'? But for this purpose I came to this hour."*

Jesus makes it plain that He knows He was sent to this world to die for it. He was sent as a sacrifice for the world, to be the seed that must go into the ground. He was sent "'til death did He part." So then Jesus steps up and tells the Father, "I'm here to do what you told me to do."

Look at verse 28:

Step Ten: The Marriage Ceremony

"'Father, glorify Your name.' Then a voice came from heaven,
saying, 'I have both glorified it and will glorify it again.'"

Jesus understood why He was sent and accepted the fact that He had to die so that many people might live. Yet even after Jesus died so that we might live, many people still choose to walk around dead. Though Jesus calls each of us to turn our backs on the world and pursue a life in Him, though He has called each of us to die to the sin of the world, He already knows that without Him we can't.

You may be walking around thinking that you're "living the life," but as long as you are not in Christ Jesus you're walking around dead. If you have not died to your sin, you are really walking around dead on Earth, dead in sin. Jesus calls for us to die to sin.

Now, dying is not an appealing thing. Jesus died on the cross, but the power of the Holy Spirit, as directed by God Almighty, raised Him from the dead. When we die to the sins of the world we, too, need to be raised from a dead state to be alive in Christ. I believe that if more people understood the joy and peace that comes with serving Jesus they might want to die to sin. If more people knew the love of Jesus, more people would want to have it. If people understood the benefits of dying, if they understood what you receive when you die to sin, that Jesus will raise you up in the same way He was raised up, more would want to follow Him.

Think of yourself as a seed that's been put in the ground. In order to live again and produce, you have to die. So you die, you're dead: what or who is going to raise you up from the dead? If you are a real seed, a combination of the sun's energy and water gives you a new body and life and raises you up. If your human body dies to sin, what or who will raise you up?

The answer is to be found in Ephesians 2:1–3: *"And you He made alive, who were dead in trespasses and sins, in which you once walked according to the course of this world, according to the prince of the power of the air, the spirit who now works in the sons of disobedience, among whom also we all once conducted ourselves in the lusts of our flesh, fulfilling the desires of the flesh and of the mind, and were by nature children of wrath, just as the others."*

God made us alive even though we were dead. It does not get any more plain than that. It is Jesus who has the power to touch you, and cause you to pay attention and to listen to His voice. It's Jesus who's calling you, even right now, into a love affair with God the Father.

Some of us were on the borderline, just dabbling in sin every now and again. For those people, it did not take too much to hear Jesus calling. For others, for people like me, we were so deep into sin that when Jesus called we couldn't hear it at first. But He loved us so much that He yelled a little louder. We were moving so fast we still didn't hear Him. So then He reached down and touched us on the shoulder, but we were having so much fun dancing with the devil that we just shrugged Him off.

Jesus loved us so much that He just wouldn't give up on us. So next time He didn't call out our name. He didn't yell. He didn't touch our shoulder. That time, because He loves us so much, He reached down and slapped us upside the head!

Step Ten: The Marriage Ceremony

He may have slapped you with a sickness. He may have slapped you with the death of a loved one. He may have slapped you with the death of a marriage. Me, He slapped with a cocaine addiction, one that brought me to my knees. One that took me so far down that I could only look up. One that made me look to the hills from which comes my help, as Psalm 121 says. One that made me understand that my help comes from the Lord.

No matter what avenue God uses, He does it that way because He loves you so. He does it that way because He predestined you to be His brother or sister. He predestined you to be like Him. Jesus wants to save you even while you're yet in your sin, because He loves you.

If you don't believe me, read it for yourself in verses 4 and 5: *"But God, who is rich in mercy, because of His great love with which He loved us, even when we were dead in trespasses, made us alive together with Christ (by grace you have been saved)."*

You see, it is the love of God that brings you from the dead. He not only wants to awaken you and make you alive, but He also wants to empower you to be all that you were born to be.

Look at verse 6: *"And raised us up together, and made us sit together in the heavenly places in Christ Jesus."*

The Bible says that God not only wants to wake you up, but He wants to raise you up together in heavenly places in Christ Jesus. That means that God not only wants you to be well to walk down here on earth, but He has also fixed it so that you will sit together with Jesus in heaven. If all that were not good enough news, the Bible suggests the reason why God does all this for you and me.

Look at verse 7: *"[T]hat in the ages to come He might show the exceeding riches of His grace in His kindness toward us in Christ Jesus."*

God touched us and made us understand that we belong to Him, and He has called on us to die to our sins. When we do, God Almighty Himself comes down and wakes us up out of our sinful state and makes us alive in Christ Jesus. Then He begins to lift us up so that we might join Christ in heavenly places, all so that He can continue to show us His loving kindness.

Jesus had to die so that He could be raised to life. He had to be the seed of life planted by death that all creation might have a chance at life eternal. It was Jesus who said of Himself, *"If I be lifted up I'll draw all men unto Me"* (John 12:32).

He had to die so that when we die to our sins, we, too, can be raised to life in Him. Nothing can break up the marriage between us and Jesus Christ, not even death. Nothing can separate us from the resurrection power of Jesus. Nothing can separate us from the healing power of Jesus. Nothing can separate us from the deliverance power of Jesus. Nothing can separate us from the love of Christ Jesus.

Look at what the Apostle Paul says about it in Romans 8:38–39: *"For I am persuaded that neither death nor life, nor angels nor principalities nor powers, nor things present nor things to come, nor height nor depth, nor any other created thing, shall be able to separate us from the love of God which is in Christ Jesus our Lord."*

Step Ten: The Marriage Ceremony

Nothing can keep you from an everlasting marriage with God the Father. Nothing—and I mean nothing—can keep you from having a love affair with God.

The marriage ceremony of salvation, coupled with a promise to love God and to permit Him to love you, allows you to enter into an intimacy with God.

Step Eleven:

Becoming One

If you are one of the blessed people who goes into a relationship the right way, by now you have gone through several steps. You began by being in the presence of your potential mate, after which you began to notice and appreciate their beauty. At that point you made a conscious decision to go after them and invite them into your space, into your life. When you invited them, they came, which gave you the opportunity to get to know them better.

While spending that time you discovered that they were as beautiful on the inside as they were fine on the outside. Realizing that you have stumbled upon something special, you decide to ask that person to join you in life. You make a lifetime commitment to them in the form of marriage. If you are blessed to have gone through these godly steps, on your wedding day you'll find great pleasure in your wedding ceremony. You will experience great delight at your wedding reception. Nothing, and I mean nothing, is going to be more important to you than consecrating your marriage.

You know what I'm talking about. You've been patient. You've had to watch that fine little something walk around you for a long time. You've dreamed about what it would be like to make love to her or him. Finally the wait is over. Now is the time the two become one. This outward expression between husband and wife is called sexual intercourse.

This physical act of the expression of love was created by God Almighty Himself, and is to this day the most exciting physical experience a husband and wife can enjoy. However, sexual intercourse between a husband and wife is but a shadow when compared to the spiritual intercourse that happens between God and mankind. If you think it's exciting making love to your husband or wife for the first time after a long wait, imagine what it is to become intimate with God the Father after such a long, long time.

Having an intimate relationship with God is similar to intercourse between a husband and wife in that it is a very personal, powerful, and bonding thing. God inserts His Holy Spirit into us and we become one with Him. That's how God makes love to us. He pours His Spirit into us, which allows us to experience Him one on one, closer than close, as intimate as one could ever imagine.

I know this may be a difficult concept for some to grasp, but Jesus Christ spent a lot of time talking about this spiritual oneness whereby He is in us and we are in Him, the two becoming one. How does this happen, and where does it begin? To experience spiritual intercourse with God you must be willing to receive the Holy Spirit. Well, what is the Holy Spirit? Before leaving the earth, Jesus promised His disciples that He would not leave them alone, but would send the comforter, helper, or the Holy Spirit to watch, teach, and lead them, and us.

John 14:15–16: *"If you love Me, keep My commandments. And I will pray the Father, and He will give you another Helper, that He may abide with you forever—"*

Jesus tells us that when He leaves, He will ask God to send us another helper—the Holy Spirit—and He, the Holy Spirit, will stay with us forever.

John 14:17 says that He is *"the Spirit of truth, whom the world cannot receive, because it neither sees Him nor knows Him; but you know Him, for He dwells with you and will be in you."* Jesus calls the helper the Spirit of truth, and goes on to say that this Spirit of truth is already with them but will soon be in them. Jesus starts talking about spiritual intercourse between Him, God, and man, through the Holy Spirit.

John 14:19–20: *"A little while longer and the world will see Me no more, but you will see Me. Because I live, you will live also. At that day you will know that I **am** in My Father, and you in Me, and I in you"* (emphasis added).

Jesus reassures us that because He lives we, too, will live eternally. But more important is how we will live once the Holy Spirit has come: *"At that day you will know that I **am** in My Father, and you in Me, and I in you"* (emphasis added).

Again, Jesus speaks about God the Father and God the Son coming inside of us to create a perfect union.

Sexual intercourse between husband and wife is for both reproduction and pleasure, but God created it more importantly for reproduction. A woman cannot create a baby without a man, and a man cannot create a baby without the woman. The two have to become one if there is to be any fruit or children from them. In the same way, God created spiritual intercourse for the intent of reproduction. It is through our union with God the Father and God the Son, through the Holy Spirit, that we too become reproductive. To better understand, let's allow Jesus to explain.

In John 15:4 He says: *"Abide in Me, and I in you. As the branch cannot bear fruit of itself, unless it abides in the vine, neither can you, unless you abide in Me."*

Jesus tells us that we cannot be reproductive without Him. He uses the analogy of a vine and a branch, and explains that it's impossible for the vine to live or be reproductive without the branch. Likewise, Jesus is saying we cannot live and or be reproductive without Him.

John 15:5: *"I am the vine, you **are** the branches. He who abides in Me, and I in him, bears much fruit; for without Me you can do nothing"* (emphasis added).

There it is! Jesus says plainly that unless we connect with Him in spiritual intimacy through the intercourse process, we can do nothing.

John 15:6: *"If anyone does not abide in Me, he is cast out as a branch and is withered; and they gather them and throw **them** into the fire, and they are burned"* (emphasis added).

Step Eleven: Becoming One

There are consequences for not being in God and not allowing God to be in you. According to scripture, any branch that is disconnected from the vine will die. Not only that but it will be burned. What is God saying to us? If we are not in Him and He in us we will be cast away to spend eternity in hell.

John 15:7: *"If you abide in Me, and My words abide in you, you will ask what you desire, and it shall be done for you."*

For those of us that take delight in a love affair with God, the Word promises that the things we ask God for, He will do for us. Understand, if you are in God and God in you, the things you ask God for will be things that line up with His will for your life.

John 16:5–7: *"But now I go away to Him who sent Me, and none of you asks Me, 'Where are You going?' But because I have said these things to you, sorrow has filled your heart. Nevertheless I tell you the truth. It is to your advantage that I go away; for if I do not go away, the Helper will not come to you; but if I depart, I will send Him to you."*

Jesus goes on to explain that it's necessary, and to our advantage, for Him to go so that the Holy Spirit can come, realizing that when it comes mankind can now enjoy not only an intimate relationship with God, but one that includes spiritual intercourse between man and God.

John 17:20: *"I do not pray for these alone, but also for those who will believe in Me through their word..."*

When Jesus says He does not "pray for these alone," He's talking about His disciples, those that would believe in Him through their word: Jesus is praying for you and me. More interesting is what He prays for us.

Look at verse 21: *"That they all may be one, as You, Father, **are** in Me, and I in You; that they also may be one in Us, that the world may believe that You sent Me"* (emphasis added).

Jesus prays that you and I would experience a rich, intimate relationship with He and God that includes us being in them and them in us in one perfect union. All this is made possible because Jesus dies on the cross and sends us the Holy Spirit to lead us into this perfect union with God.

The Holy Spirit is key to us developing a love affair with God. It's so important that God gives it to us freely. It's a gift from God, as Luke 11:13 makes clear: *"If you then, being evil, know how to give good gifts to your children, how much more will your heavenly Father give the Holy Spirit to those who ask Him!"*

This scripture tells us that our God wants to give us the gift of the Holy Spirit that draws us into perfect relationship with Him. This is no ordinary gift and, quite frankly, is the greatest one that has ever been given to man. It's a good gift: the very Word of God says so in James 1:16–17: *"Do not be deceived, my beloved brethren. Every good gift and every perfect gift is from above, and comes down from the Father of lights, with whom there is no variation or shadow of turning."*

So, if it's a good gift, then we understand without question that it is a gift that comes from the Lord. This gift has characteristics like no other. It gives light in darkness and hope to the hopeless. It provides a father to the fatherless, a mother to the motherless, and a friend to the lonely. This gift is like milk for the corn flakes, ketchup for the hot dog, and vanilla ice cream on the apple pie. It's a gift that keeps on giving; it never ever stops.

Let's see how Jesus describes this gift in John 4:7–9: *"A woman of Samaria came to draw water. Jesus said to her, 'Give Me a drink.' For His disciples had gone away into the city to buy food. Then the woman of Samaria said to Him, 'How is it that You, being a Jew, ask a drink from me, a Samaritan woman?' For Jews have no deal-ings with Samaritans."*

If we knew what God wants to give us through the Holy Spirit, we would go running to Him.

Samaritans were half-Jew, half-Gentile people. They were an outcast people. They were pagan worshipers and an enemy of the Jewish people. This Samaritan woman realizes that a Jewish man is talking to her. She knows that this is not a normal thing. She knows that custom dictates that she's not worthy to even talk to him. This man Jesus is not supposed to be talking to her. (As a side note, I'm so glad I serve a Jesus that does not mind stopping and talking to outcast people like me!)

Now look at verse 10: *"Jesus answered and said to her, 'If you knew the gift of God, and who it is who says to you, "Give Me a drink," you would have asked Him, and He would have given you living water.'"*

Jesus says, *"If you knew the gift of God."* If she knew what God wanted to give, she would ask Him for it. Then Jesus says if she knew who was there to give it to her, she would ask Him for it.

The same applies to you and me today: If we really knew who it is that we deal with when we deal with God, we would act a little differently. If we knew what God wants to give us through the Holy Spirit, we would go running to Him to ask for the gift.

What is God trying to tell us? "If you knew what I was trying to give you, if you knew it was Me, God, trying to give it to you. If you knew how badly I want to give it to you. If you knew how much I've already sacrificed for you to have it. If you knew just how much I love you. If you knew, you would have asked Me for the gift of the Holy Spirit and I would gladly give it to you."

In His encounter with the Samaritan woman Jesus tells us what the gift is. He calls it living water, water that's alive. Well, what is this living water?

Look at verse 11: *"The woman said to Him, 'Sir, You have nothing to draw with, and the well is deep. Where then do You get that living water?'"*

This woman immediately thinks that the living water is something she can draw from the well. She thinks it is a new kind of water that just came on the market. How do we know? Look at what she says in verse 12: *"Are You greater than our father Jacob, who gave us the well, and drank from it himself, as well as his sons and his livestock?"*

Now look at how Jesus responds, in verse 13: *"Jesus answered and said to her, 'Whoever drinks of this water will thirst again.'"*

Jesus says if you drink from this well, if you drink this water, you'll thirst again because it's physical water. The woman does not yet understand that Jesus is not talking about the physical, but instead the spiritual.

In verse 14 He continues: *"... but whoever drinks of the water that I shall give him will never thirst. But the water that I shall give him will become in him a fountain of water springing up into everlasting life."*

Jesus says of the water He is offering you today, if you drink of it you'll never thirst again because it's spiritual water. Jesus tells us that the gift from God is living water, and this living water will become in us a fountain of water springing up into everlasting life.

The living water that Jesus is talking about is the Holy Spirit. Through the power of the Holy Spirit we will receive eternal life. The Holy Spirit is the life source, the power that leads us into eternal life. It is a spiritual water that allows you to commune with God in an intimate way. It's a gift that God will insert inside of you that will lead you to an awesome love affair with Him, as well as eternal life.

If you don't believe me read it for yourself in Romans 6:23: *"For the wages of sin **is** death, but the gift of God **is** eternal life in Christ Jesus our Lord"* (emphasis added).

The gift of the Holy Spirit will lead you to a life eternal with God. That means we will not die, but instead transition into everlasting life, a life without end. God wants to make love to you right now.

Step Twelve:

Spiritual Climax

When a husband and wife make love, each is committed to helping the other achieve the ultimate climax. This is the climactic point of intercourse when the body and the mind experience a pleasurable wave of sensations. Just as God designed our bodies to enjoy a physical climax, He gave us the ability to experience spiritual exhilaration in our relationship with Him. So that we are clear, spiritual intercourse occurs when God's Holy Spirit comes inside of you. Once inside, this spirit allows you to experience God in new and exciting ways. This Holy Spirit allows you to see and feel spiritual things that would not be possible unless God be in you. Every person will experience a different form of spiritual climax. Studies have shown that many people have difficulty achieving sexual climax, but not so with God. Each and every person who seeks out a love affair with God can experience His spiritual presence. There are varying ways that God allows us to experience Him, and varying levels of intensity.

The feelings that are hoped for between husband and wife while making love are guaranteed in spiritual intercourse with God. You will be able to have multiple climaxes. That's right, your climactic experiences with God will never stop. As soon as you're done experiencing a climax on one day with the Lord, He immediately sets up your next climactic experience. As soon as you're done experiencing a climax in one season of your life, God allows you to begin preparation for another climax in the next. As you continue having intercourse with God, He allows you to experience Him in new and exciting ways, through your life experiences, day after day, month after month, year after year!

How people experience God's presence can be hard to put into words. God moves on every individual in a personal kind of way. Some, while having a spiritual climax, are filled with emotions that bring them to tears. Some are so overwhelmed with the sure power of God that they become physically slain, whereby they are so overcome they actually faint. Some who are completely filled with His Spirit begin to shout, praise, and exhort Him. Again, the experiences are so vast and different that it's impossible to explain. However, we do have a recorded account of man's first experience with God's Holy Spirit.

Acts 1:4–5: *"And being assembled together with them, He commanded them not to depart from Jerusalem, but to wait for the Promise of the Father, 'which,' He said, 'you have heard from Me; for John truly baptized with water, but you shall be baptized with the Holy Spirit not many days from now.'"*

This is Jesus explaining to His disciples that a plan has been put into place that will allow man to experience Him and God the Father in extraordinary ways. This strategy includes God entering into man through the Holy Spirit. Jesus tells His disciples to wait for the Promise of the Father, which He later explains is the gift of the Holy Spirit.

Acts 2:1: *"When the Day of Pentecost had fully come, they were all with one accord in one place."*

The book of Acts records that the disciples of Jesus were of "one accord," meaning they were all in one place, waiting for one thing. The thing they were waiting for was the fulfillment of the promise from Jesus. Acts 2:2–4: *"And suddenly there came a sound from heaven, as of a rushing mighty wind, and it filled the whole house where they were sitting. Then there appeared to them divided tongues, as of fire, and one sat upon each of them. And they were all filled with the Holy Spirit and began to speak with other tongues, as the Spirit gave them utterance."*

When a husband and wife are making love and a climax is achieved by either of them, it's felt on the inside. However, there is an outward expression of that sensational feeling. Both the husband and the wife might experience ejaculation, whereby fluids are ejected from their sexual organs. These are outward expressions of the internal climax they just achieved. Spiritual climax works in the same manner. There is usually an outward expression of the inward experience of spiritual intercourse between God and man. We witness this in the account in Acts. Look again at verses 2–4: *"And suddenly there came a sound from heaven, as of a rushing mighty wind, and it filled the whole house where they were sitting. Then there appeared to them divided tongues, as of fire, and one sat upon each of them. And they were all filled with the Holy Spirit and began to speak with other tongues, as the Spirit gave them utterance."* Once they were filled in the inside, an expression came to the outside in the form of them speaking in tongues. An explanation of "tongues" here would take us way off track; the point is that whenever God comes into us, whenever we have intercourse with God, we will experience an orgasm. This climax will produce some type of outward expression.

Such was the case with the psalmist in Psalm 63:1: *"O God, You are my God; early will I seek You; my soul thirsts for You; my flesh longs for You in a dry and thirsty land where there is no water."*

Here the psalmist speaks like a man longing for the touch of his wife. However the "touching" he's really looking for is that of God. The writer begins by saying, *"My soul longs for you."* That means the very core of his being was crying out for God. Obviously the person had experienced God in a way that was so amazing he just wanted more.

The verse goes on to say, *"My flesh longs for you."* This would indicate that through spiritual intimacy with God, this person's very physical body was satisfied.

Verse 2: *"So I have looked for You in the sanctuary, to see Your power and Your glory."*

Because he has tasted the love of God and experienced Him in an intimate way, this person now searches for Him, wanting to taste His power, wanting to see His glory. Then he tells us why. Verse 3 reads: *"Because Your lovingkindness is better than life, my lips shall praise You."*

He proclaims God's love is better than life. Wow, what an experience he must have had! As a result he goes on to say, *"My lips shall praise you."* The only reason a human being would praise another has to be because they have done something very special for them. It's obvious that God has done something very special, and as a result this person wants to tell the world about it.

An intimate experience with God leads to climactic expressions for what He's done.

Look at verses 4–5: *"Thus I will bless You while I live; I will lift up my hands in Your name. My soul shall be satisfied as with marrow and fatness, and my mouth shall praise You with joyful lips."*

These are sounds of one that has been satisfied by God Almighty Himself, and as a result he now expresses climactic praise for what God has done.

The Bible records many such events, where an intimate experience with God leads to climactic expressions for what He's done. Such was the case with one of God's great prophets, as he was so filled with God's Word that he could not even control his mouth.

Jeremiah 20:7–8: *"O Lord, You induced me, and I was persuaded; You are stronger than I, and have prevailed. I am in derision daily; everyone mocks me. For when I spoke, I cried out; I shouted, 'Violence and plunder!' Because the word of the Lord was made to me a reproach and a derision daily."*

Jeremiah reported a climactic experience where God placed His Word in him through the Holy Spirit. As a result, Jeremiah began to cry out to the people. He began to shout out God's instructions to the people. When he did this, the Bible reports that the people began to laugh and scorn Jeremiah. Look at what happened next (verse 9): *"Then I said, 'I will not make mention of Him, nor speak anymore in His name.' But His word was in my heart like a burning fire shut up in my bones; I was weary of holding it back, and I could not."*

Jeremiah decided not to talk about God anymore, but because he was caught up in God, because God was moving in him, he experienced a climax that would not allow him to stop talking about God. Jeremiah explains it by saying it was "like a burning fire shut up in my bones." It was uncontrollable!

During the days Jesus walked the earth, there were many recorded climactic experiences where people were physically touched by Him and immediately experienced unbelievable spiritual highs that resulted in their bodies being changed or healed.

Luke 13:10–13: *"Now He was teaching in one of the synagogues on the Sabbath. And behold, there was a woman who had a spirit of infirmity eighteen years, and was bent over and could in no way raise herself up. But when Jesus saw her, He called her to Him and said to her, 'Woman, you are loosed from your infirmity.' And He laid His hands on her, and immediately she was made straight, and glorified God."*

This woman who was afflicted, once touched by Jesus, once He sent His Holy Spirit through her, immediately was healed and began to glorify God—an outward expression of the inward spiritual experience that led to her healing.

On many occasions Jesus physically touched a person and released His Holy Spirit into them. However, there is one example of Jesus having spiritual intercourse with someone where He needed only to speak to him. Jesus displayed the power to speak His Spirit into an individual and because of it the person experienced the climax of a lifetime.

Look at John 11: 1–7: *"Now a certain man was sick, Lazarus of Bethany, the town of Mary and her sister Martha. It was that Mary who anointed the Lord with fragrant oil and wiped His feet with her hair, whose brother Lazarus was sick. Therefore the sisters sent to Him, saying, 'Lord, behold, he whom You love is sick.' When Jesus heard that, He said, 'This sickness is not unto death, but for the glory of God, that the Son of God may be glorified through it.' Now Jesus loved Martha and her sister and Lazarus. So, when He heard that he was sick, He stayed two more days in the place where He was. Then after this He said to the disciples, 'Let us go to Judea again.'"*

Jesus finds out that His good friend Lazarus is very sick. Lazarus's sisters, Martha and Mary, send word to Jesus to come, fast. The Bible reports that Jesus stays away for an additional two days.

Look at verses 17–23: *"So when Jesus came, He found that he had already been in the tomb four days. Now Bethany was near Jerusalem, about two miles away. And many of the Jews had joined the women around Martha and Mary, to comfort them concerning their brother. Now Martha, as soon as she heard that Jesus was coming, went and met Him, but Mary was sitting in the house. Now Martha said to Jesus, 'Lord, if You had been here, my brother would not have died. But even now I know that whatever You ask of God, God will give You.' Jesus said to her, 'Your brother will rise again.'"*

Jesus finally nears the home of His sick friend, only to be met by Martha. Jesus tells her: *"Your brother will rise again."*

Look at verses 38–39: *"Then Jesus, again groaning in Himself, came to the tomb. It was a cave, and a stone lay against it. Jesus said, 'Take away the stone.' Martha, the sister of him who was dead, said to Him, 'Lord, by this time there is a stench, for he has been dead four days.'"*

The body of Lazarus has been in the tomb for four days, yet even now Jesus assures them that Lazarus will live again.

John 11:40–44: *"Jesus said to her, 'Did I not say to you that if you would believe you would see the glory of God?' Then they took away the stone from the place where the dead man was lying. And Jesus lifted up His eyes and said, 'Father, I thank You that You have heard Me. And I know that You always hear Me, but because of the people who are standing by I said this, that they may believe that You sent Me.' Now when He had said these things, He cried with a loud voice, 'Lazarus, come forth!' And he who had died came out bound hand and foot with grave clothes, and his face was wrapped with a cloth. Jesus said to them, 'Loose him, and let him go.'"*

Notice that, with His voice alone, Jesus sends His spirit into Lazarus. Jesus has spiritual intercourse with Lazarus. Lazarus experiences a spiritual climax, which is manifested in the outward expression of him being raised to life, though he has been dead for four days.

Just as the Holy Spirit provided life for Lazarus, it is the desire of God that you too experience life—eternal life, that is, available for you if you will allow yourself to have a love affair with God.

This leads us to what I believe to be the greatest spiritual opportunity God has given man. It is the greatest way a person can engage in spiritual intercourse and have a spiritual climax with God. To better understand it, we need to go back to the book of Acts, right after man has experienced the move of the Holy Spirit for the first time.

Acts 2:36–7: *"'Therefore let all the house of Israel know assuredly that God has made this Jesus, whom you crucified, both Lord and Christ.' Now when they heard this, they were cut to the heart, and said to Peter and the rest of the apostles, 'Men and brethren, what shall we do?'"*

After Peter and the rest of the disciples receive the Holy Spirit, Peter—who was once filled with fear, and even denied knowing Jesus Christ—is now empowered by the Holy Spirit and steps up to preach to the thousands of men in attendance. He shares the story of Jesus Christ and they are touched at the heart, asking Peter and the other disciples what they should do.

Look at Peter's answer to them (verses 38–39): *"Then Peter said to them, 'Repent, and let every one of you be baptized in the name of Jesus Christ for the remission of sins; and you shall receive the gift of the Holy Spirit. For the promise is to you and to your children, and to all who are afar off, as many as the Lord our God will call.'"* Peter tells them to repent and receive Jesus Christ as their Lord and Savior. He also promises that they, too, will be filled with the Holy Spirit. Let's see how they respond (verses 40–41): *"And with many other words he testified and exhorted them, saying, 'Be saved from this perverse generation.' Then those who gladly received his word were baptized; and that day about three thousand souls were added to them."*

Empowered by the Holy Spirit, Peter is no longer afraid, but is now a powerful spokesperson representing the gospel of Jesus Christ. Peter's boldness is the outward expression of the Holy Spirit working on the inside of him, as he and God are now engaged in spiritual intercourse.

This results in Peter experiencing a spiritual climax which manifests itself as power and boldness to speak God's Word. As a result, the Bible records that about three thousand people also received salvation and began their own intimate relationships with God. God chose to have spiritual intercourse with each of them.

The outward expression for these three thousand souls is not documented; however, we can expect that their lives changed in a very dramatic and profound way. When you allow God to come inside of you, there is absolutely no way you can remain the same. Your life becomes a life which shadows the very Spirit of God. Your behavior honors God and loves people. When we come into Christ Jesus, we take off the old man and put on a new man.

2 Corinthians 5:17 says: *"Therefore, if anyone **is** in Christ, **he is** a new creation; old things have passed away; behold, all things have become new"* (emphasis added).

Step Twelve: Spiritual Climax

This scripture supports the notion that it's impossible to remain the same person you were before God comes inside of you. We can get a real good picture of what we should look like after having an encounter with God by merely looking at His Word.

Colossians 3:5–7 says: *"Therefore put to death your members which are on the earth: fornication, uncleanness, passion, evil desire, and covetousness, which is idolatry. Because of these things the wrath of God is coming upon the sons of disobedience, in which you yourselves once walked when you lived in them."*

This scripture suggests we put off the things of old we walked and lived in before we came to know God. It goes on to name the negative attitudes we must allow God to help us get rid of.

Verses 8–10: *"But now you yourselves are to put off all these: anger, wrath, malice, blasphemy, filthy language out of your mouth. Do not lie to one another, since you have put off the old man with his deeds, and have put on the new man who is renewed in knowledge according to the image of Him who created him."*

You can clearly see there is a very definite change in the new person who has connected with God through Jesus Christ. Just as there are very specific things that must come off in your new relationship with God, there are some things that you must put on.

Look at verses 12–13: *"Therefore, as the elect of God, holy and beloved, put on tender mercies, kindness, humility, meekness, longsuffering; bearing with one another, and forgiving one another, if anyone has a complaint against another; even as Christ forgave you, so you also must do."*

The scripture suggests you put on the very essence of God, which includes mercy, kindness, and forgiveness. But there is something that is more important than these, which actually encompasses them and more.

Verses 14–15: *"But above all these things put on love, which is the bond of perfection. And let the peace of God rule in your hearts, to which also you were called in one body; and be thankful."*

This leads us to what I believe is the greatest outward expression of spiritual intercourse between God and man.

Look at Matthew 1:18: *"Now the birth of Jesus Christ was as follows: After His mother Mary was betrothed to Joseph, before they came together, she was found with child of the Holy Spirit."*

The scripture tells us that a virgin girl named Mary was found "with a child of the Holy Spirit," which means it was the Holy Spirit's child. This also means the Holy Spirit must have had spiritual intercourse with Mary. How else could they have conceived a baby?

The Bible makes plain that Mary was betrothed to Joseph before they came together, which means they were engaged to be married. The next part of the verse says "before they came together," which means before they had sex. That's right: they were engaged and had never had sex, but nevertheless Mary was pregnant.

I'm sure you understand that this was a problematic situation. I don't know many men who would believe that their fiancée is still a virgin, as she claims, when she is already pregnant!

Step Twelve: Spiritual Climax

Look at verse 19: *"Then Joseph her husband, being a just **man**, and not wanting to make her a public example, was minded to put her away secretly"* (emphasis added).

The Bible says that Joseph was a good man, but because of this situation he was minded to put Mary away secretly. There are a lot of different arguments as to why he would want to do this. Some would say to protect her, others would argue to protect himself from being a laughing stock. Nevertheless, he was minded to put her away.

Look at verse 20: *"But while he thought about these things, behold, an angel of the Lord appeared to him in a dream, saying, 'Joseph, son of David, do not be afraid to take to you Mary your wife, for that which is conceived in her is of the Holy Spirit.'"* What things was Joseph thinking about? It must have been this crazy situation he was in. He had a wife that he'd never touched, yet she was pregnant. Then God steps in to make him understand that it is a "God thing" that's going on. God does it so that Joseph does not go off and do something stupid in the midst of God's move in his and Mary's life.

There's a message here for you and me. When you find yourself dealing with a situation that you just can't seem to understand or comprehend, when you are faced with a situation that is beyond your ability to figure out, God will step in and make it clear. That is, if you will let Him.

Look at verse 21: *"And she will bring forth a Son, and you shall call His name Jesus, for He will save His people from their sins."*

God tells Joseph that Mary will have a child and Joseph will call Him Jesus. God tells Joseph what He has done. He tells Joseph that He, God Almighty, has had intercourse with his wife. I don't know about you, but that would have simply blown my mind!

God not only tells Joseph what He's done, but He also explains why He did it. God says He did it so that Jesus will be born and save His people. There is one more reason why this "God thing" needs to happen this way.

Look at verses 22–23: *"So all this was done that it might be fulfilled which was spoken by the Lord through the prophet, saying:* ***'Behold, the virgin shall be with child, and bear a Son, and they shall call His name Immanuel,'*** *which is translated, 'God with us'"* (emphasis added).

That one more reason is because God had already said it would happen that way. He said it through one of the great prophets, 733 years before Jesus was ever born.

Look at Isaiah 7:14: *"Therefore the LORD Himself will give you a sign: Behold, the virgin shall conceive and bear a Son, and shall call His name Immanuel."*

The story of the Virgin Mary did not just fall from the sky. The birth of Jesus did not come by happenstance. You need to know that God put a plan in place for you thousands of years ago.

God knew you were going to need a Savior. God knew that man was going to be in trouble, and because He loves you so much, seven hundred years before Jesus was conceived, God said it was going to happen. God said a virgin shall give birth to the Savior.

Step Twelve: Spiritual Climax

God also knew that you and I would be here today, considering spiritual climax and how this story is the greatest example of God's Holy Spirit going inside a human being, having intercourse, and experiencing the greatest climax known to man. Remember, there is usually an outward expression of the inward experience of spiritual intercourse between God and man. The Bible tells us that the birth of Jesus came as a result of a spiritual intercourse between the Holy Spirit and the Virgin Mary. The climactic result was Jesus the Christ being born.

The same experience God had with the Virgin Mary is the very same that God wants you to have today. God desires to have a love affair with you. He wants to see you operate in the fullness of His power, which can only be obtained through an intimate relationship with Him. It's there that you become one with Him through the Holy Spirit.

God promises that if you will take a chance on Him, not only will He give you these things, but He promises to give them to you always and forever.

Afterword:

"Always and Forever"

I was recently reintroduced to a song that was one of my favorites as a teenager growing up in Rochester, New York: "Always and Forever," performed by the R&B group, Heat Wave. I say reintroduced because when I heard the song this time it sounded different.

You see, when I listened to it back in high school my thoughts were all about that pretty girl that I wanted to be my girlfriend. "Always and Forever" was that special love song for the young man and young woman who thought they were "oh so in love." To me, it beautifully described the feelings between two people.

When I heard it again not long ago, I discovered that it was, indeed, a beautiful love song; however, the love relationship now was not between a man and a woman but instead between me and my God.

Here are some of the lyrics:

> Every day love me your own special way
> Melt all my heart away with a smile
> Take time to tell me you really care
> And we'll share tomorrow together
> I'll always love you forever

These lyrics now seem to cry out to me in a special way. I hear God saying to me: Every day love me your own special way, melt all my heart away with a smile. I hear Him saying: Take time to tell me you really care and we'll share tomorrow together; I'll always love you forever.

The love of God is always and forever.

The things of God are always and forever. The love of God is always and forever. However, this promise of always and forever is a two-way street. God says He will be there always and forever, but you, too, must make the commitment to stay with God always and forever. God wants you to know that you, too, can have a love affair with Him that will last always and forever. To help you understand this a little better, God has provided some guidance and examples in His Word.

First let's examine our responsibility to love and obey God always.

Deuteronomy 11:1: *"Therefore you shall love the Lord your God, and keep His charge, His statutes, His judgments, and His commandments **always***" (emphasis added).

As a part of your commitment to the relationship between you and God, you must commit to loving Him and keeping His charge to you to honor all of His statutes, judgments, and commandments. We must commit to doing them always. When we commit to God, God commits to us.

Afterword: "Always and Forever"

Acts 2:25: *"For David says concerning Him: 'I foresaw the Lord **always** before my face, for He is at my right hand, that I may not be shaken'"* (emphasis added).

King David proclaims that God was before his face always, and that He was at his right hand throughout his life, so that he would be able to stand strong. God promises to do the same for you. Not only does God promise to stand with you, He also promises to go ahead to lead you.

2 Corinthians 2:14: *"Now thanks be to God who **always** leads us in triumph in Christ, and through us diffuses the fragrance of His knowledge in every place"* (emphasis added).

This scripture clearly makes you understand that God will always lead you in the way of righteousness and provide you with godly knowledge. To say that God will always be with you is to also say Jesus will always be with you.

Matthew 28:18–20: *"And Jesus came and spoke to them, saying, 'All authority has been given to Me in heaven and on earth. Go therefore and make disciples of all the nations, baptizing them in the name of the Father and of the Son and of the Holy Spirit, teaching them to observe all things that I have commanded you; and lo, I am with you always, even to the end of the age"* (emphasis added).

Just as He is about to leave the earth, Jesus gives us a final instruction. He tells us to go into the world and make disciples of all nations. That is, to tell the world about the love of God the Father, God the Son, and God the Holy Spirit. Then Jesus promises us that He will be with us always, even to the end of the age. What an awesome promise! Just as God promises to be with you always, He also promises His Word will be with you forever.

1 Peter 1:22–25: *"Since you have purified your souls in obeying the truth through the Spirit in sincere love of the brethren, love one another fervently with a pure heart, having been born again, not of corruptible seed but incorruptible, through the word of God which lives and abides **forever**, because 'All flesh is as grass, and all the glory of man as the flower of the grass. The grass withers, and its flower falls away, but the word of the Lord endures **forever**.' Now this is the word which by the gospel was preached to you"* (emphasis added).

Just as the Word of God will be with you forever, so will His Holy Spirit be with you forever.

John 14:15–17: *"If you love Me, keep My commandments. And I will pray the Father, and He will give you another Helper, that He may abide with you forever—the Spirit of truth, whom the world cannot receive, because it neither sees Him nor knows Him; but you know Him, for He dwells with you and will be in you."*

The reason God promises that He is going to be with you always and forever is because He Himself will reign forever.

Exodus 15:18: *"The Lord shall reign forever and ever."*

This promise of always and forever will not come easy. There will be difficulties that will arise to test your commitment to God. He is only interested in relationships that are real, meaning He wants to engage with someone who will truly love Him to the best of their ability. God does not want the person who runs at the first sight of adversity but instead someone who is willing to go "through the fire, to the limits, and to the wall."

These are not original sentiments. The words come from a song by another great R&B singer, Chaka Khan. Written in 1984, the song is about a woman who falls in love with a man who has trust issues. He wants to take it slow and play it smart, but she's ready to go all the way.

The chorus of this song says, "Through the fire, to the limit, to the wall. For a chance to be with you, I'd gladly risk it all." Then it continues, "Through the fire, through whatever, come what may. For a chance at loving you, I'd take it all the way. Right down to the wire, even through the fire."

You see, the song talks about a love beyond loves. It has to be for this person to say she'd be willing to go through anything as long as she can be with him. Well, God is looking for a few good men and women who will love Him like that. Not just any ordinary love. God is talking about an extraordinary love. He is looking for the loves of His life.

God wants you to know that He'll know those who really love Him because they will be the ones who love God through the fire. They will love God to the limit, and they will love God to the wall. Without hesitation, this kind of person will stand up and say, "For a chance to be with you, God, to be with you, Jesus, I'd gladly risk it all." God says He'll know if you're His true love because you'll say, "Through whatever, come what may, for a chance at loving you, God, I'd take it all the way, right to down to the wire, even through the fire."

Will you love Him through fire? Will you love Him when He takes you to your limits? Will love Him when it feels like life has your back against the wall? Let's take a quick look at some people who really loved God that way.

Psalm 66:8–9: *"Oh, bless our God, you peoples! And make the voice of His praise to be heard, who keeps our soul among the living, and does not allow our feet to be moved."*

These are people who are pleased with God! They talk about a God who blesses them. They talk about praising His name. They declare that He keeps their soul among the living, that He is a God that does not allow their feet to be moved. Why is it that they love Him so?

Look at what follows in verse 10: *"For You, O God, have tested us; You have refined us as silver is refined."*

These people have gone through the fire. The writer says God has refined them as silver is refined. Through Jesus, God will refine you as silver is refined. How is that done? With fire. All the impurities are burned away, so that the only thing left is pure silver.

First, the silver is put in a smelting pot and placed over burning fire until all the impurities float to the top. The silversmith knows that the silver is pure when he can see his reflection in it. In the same way, God Almighty is the refiner of souls. After He has allowed us to simmer in the fire of life, He looks into our souls to see if He can see His reflection in us.

Afterword: "Always and Forever"

How do I know this? Look at Malachi 3:3: *"He will sit as a refiner and a purifier of silver; He will purify the sons of Levi, and purge them as gold and silver, that they may offer to the Lord an offering in righteousness."*

God is the purifier of our souls. It's through His refining process that we are fully developed as His children.

Now look at Psalm 66:11: *"You brought us into the net; You laid affliction on our backs."*

These are people who are to the limits. Anything or anyone caught in a net can't go anywhere; they are at the disposal of whoever is holding the net. God is holding the net of your life and though it may appear painful, it is the very thing that will bless and empower you.

How do I know?

Look at the next two verses in the psalm: *"You have caused men to ride over our heads; we went through fire and through water; but You brought us out to rich fulfillment."*

These are the people who have been to the wall. But we can understand why they loved God the way they did.

Notice that God didn't just bring them out of their difficult circumstances, He brought them out in rich fulfillment. The same way He brought them out, He'll bring you out—that is, if you will trust Him.

Which brings me to the question, who would not want to have a relationship with a God that is so loving and caring? Who would not want to have a love affair with the being who created love?

When you realize that God is best thing that could ever happen to you, that's when you are ready to walk down the aisle of life and dedicate your life to Him in marriage.

For those of you who are ready to marry God, there is a vow that you must be willing to make. The decision to make this vow is the most important one you will make in your life. This is truly a life-or-death decision. If you choose God today, you're choosing ever-lasting life with Him. To say no to God is to say yes to everlasting death and suffering.

As I have said previously, this vow, like any other marriage vow, must be said out loud.

Romans 10:8–10 explains why: *"But what does it say? 'The word is near you, in your mouth and in your heart' (that is, the word of faith which we preach): that if you confess with your mouth the Lord Jesus and believe in your heart that God has raised Him from the dead, you will be saved. For with the heart one believes unto righteousness, and with the mouth confession is made unto salvation."*

This passage tells us that if you confess with your mouth and believe in your heart that Jesus Christ is the Son of God who died for your sins, you will be saved. In other words, you will be married to God, ready to live the fulfilling life He purposed for you.

Are you ready? Here's what you can say:

Afterword: "Always and Forever"

Dear God,
    Thank you for the conviction of my heart
    To receive Jesus Christ as my personal Savior.
    I believe that Jesus is the Son of God
    Who died on the cross
    To save me from sin.
    I also believe God raised Jesus from the dead.
    Jesus, come into my heart right now.
    Thank you, Father, for loving me and saving me through
        the power of your Holy Spirit.
    Amen!

If you just said this prayer, welcome to the family of God, to the Body of Christ! I pray that you will quickly attach yourself to a Bible-believing church, so that you might be properly discipled.

I also want to invite you to join me and others as we fight for the rights of Jesus Christ in a "Back to God" movement. Please go to www.b2god.com for more information.

May God bless you and may God keep you.

About the Author

Evangelist, author, educator and international speaker **DEXTER SANDERS** has a unique gift for sharing the love of Christ, which has resulted in thousands across the country and abroad receiving Jesus as their Lord and Savior. Dexter travels the globe sharing the good news through church events, festivals, concerts and community outreaches. In addition, Dexter is a gifted character education speaker for middle and high schools across the nation, sharing a message of values along with suicide and bullying prevention.

IF YOU'RE A FAN OF THIS BOOK, PLEASE TELL OTHERS

- Write a positive review on www.amazon.com.

- Purchase additional copies to give away as gifts.

- Suggest *Soulmate* to friends.

- Write about *Soulmate* on your blog. Post excerpts to your social media sites such as: Facebook, Twitter, Pinterest, Instagram, etc.

- When you're in a bookstore, ask if they carry the book. The book is available through all major distributors, so any bookstore that does not have it in stock can easily order it.

You can order additional copies of the book from my website as well as in bookstores by going to **www.b2god.com**. Special bulk quantity discounts are available.